C000174921

ENNISKERRY

ENNISKERRY
A HISTORY

MICHAEL SEERY

The History Press Ireland

In loving memory of Bridget 'Birdie' Seery 1910–1995

First published 2011

The History Press Ireland
119 Lower Baggot Street
Dublin 2
Ireland
www.thehistorypress.ie

© Michael Seery, 2011

British Library Cataloguing in Publication Data.
A catalogue record for this book is available from the British Library.

ISBN 978 1 84588 699 8

Typesetting and origination by The History Press
Printed in Malta

CONTENTS

ACKNOWLEDGEMENTS

I would like to acknowledge a number of people and institutions whose help and guidance made this book possible. The material which forms the basis of this book is archival in nature, and I would like to thank the staff at the National Archives of Ireland and Mr Paul Ferguson of the Map Library, Trinity College Dublin for their help in sourcing information. I would like to thank Dublin City Library for their resources and the Ordnance Survey of Ireland for providing access to their historic maps archive.

I wish to especially thank the National Library of Ireland and its staff. The generosity with time and help and the materials sourced by librarians at the National Library have had an enormous impact on this work. Particular thanks go to Ms Honora Faul, Prints and Drawings Department, the Duty Librarians and staff in the Main Reading Room, the Duty Archivists and staff in the Manuscripts Department and the Curator and staff, especially Mr Keith Murphy, at the National Photographic Archive, who kindly released a photographic album from exhibition for viewing. The National Library also provided access to the House of Commons Parliamentary Papers, Powerscourt parish records and nineteenth-century newspapers.

As an amateur local historian, I am indebted to the expertise of professional historians, shared so readily through helpful publications. In particular, the Maynooth Research Guides for Irish Local History were invaluable to me in my research, especially those by E. Margaret Crawford (*Counting the People*), Susan M. Parkes (*A Guide to Sources for the History of Irish Education, 1780-1922*), Jacinta Prunty (*Maps and Map-Making in Local History*) and C.J. Woods (*Travellers' Accounts as Source-Materials for Irish Historians*). In addition, the work of J.H. Andrews (*A Paper Landscape*), Liam Clare (*The Bray and Enniskerry Railway*), Terence Dooley (*The Decline of the Big House in Ireland*), Ken

Hannigan and William Nolan (*Wicklow: History and Society*), Antonia McManus (*The Irish Hedge School and its Books*) and Niall O'Ciosain (*Print and Popular Culture in Ireland 1750–1850*) all provided me with very useful context. I am very grateful to Michael Fewer (*The Wicklow Military Road*) and William Hogg (*The Millers and Mills of Ireland of about 1850*) for their correspondence and for sharing their expertise.

Finally, I would like to thank Niall, my parents, family and friends. This was never meant to be a book at all, and the fact that it became one is due to their generous moral support.

To find out more and share your history, see www.enniskerryhistory.org.

NOTE ON SPELLING
OF PLACE NAMES

Place names are given according to how they appear on Ordnance Survey maps except where the source referred to uses an alternative spelling, in which case the alternative spelling is used with the place name in quotation marks.

1

A SENSE OF PLACE

Overview – Development of the village 1760–1823 – Ongoing Development
1823–1901 – Summary

OVERVIEW

The origins of a settlement at Enniskerry can be traced back to at least the sixteenth century with one of the earliest references given by Liam Price, who refers to a place called 'Anakery' in his book *Place Names of County Wicklow*.[1] Enniskerry was laid out in its current form in the first half of the nineteenth century, with much of the development at this time leaving the legacy of the layout as we know it today – including the construction of roads, houses, churches and schools. The Town Clock was constructed in 1843 to mark the centenary of the creation of the Viscountcy of Powerscourt in 1744.[2] The purpose of this chapter is to discuss the development of the village following completion of the new house at Powerscourt around 1741 through the remainder of the eighteenth and nineteenth centuries.

For this purpose, evidence is collected from a variety of contemporary sources including maps, the Ordnance Survey and Land Valuation projects, information from travel literature, archive images, as well as material from the Powerscourt papers. As the estate village of Powerscourt, the development of Enniskerry was dependent on the ambitions, ideas and finances of the Viscount, and each of them had a role at various stages of development. There were also two long minorities (1823–1833, 1844–1854) owing to early deaths of two Viscounts (Table 1) during which the estate was administered by guardians. It is useful to align the development of the village to lifetimes of various Viscounts – initial establishment of the village and early development up to death of the fifth Viscount in 1823; substantial development during the short lifetime of the 6th Viscount and the minority of the 7th Viscount, culminating in the planning and development of two churches in the village in the early 1860s; and a period of continuance over the long life of the 7th Viscount, which saw life in the village change very little over the remainder of the century.

Table 1: Periods of the Viscountcy of Powerscourt (3rd Creation)

	Name	Born	Viscountcy	Died
1st	Richard	19-8-1697	4-2-1744	21-10-1751
2nd	Edward	23-10-1729	21-10-1751	6-5-1764
3rd	Richard	24-12-1730	6-5-1764	8-8-1788
4th	Richard	29-8-1762	8-8-1788	19-7-1809
5th	Richard	11-9-1790	19-7-1809	9-8-1823
6th	Richard	18-1-1815	9-8-1823 (minor)	11-8-1844
7th	Mervyn Edward	13-10-1836	11-8-1844 (minor)	5-6-1904
8th	Mervyn Richard	16-7-1880	5-6-1904	21-3-1947
9th	Mervyn Patrick	22-8-1905	21-3-1947	3-4-1973
10th	Mervyn Niall	3-9-1935	3-4-1973	

DEVELOPMENT OF THE VILLAGE 1760–1823

Rocque's Map and the Settlement at Enniskerry

The period 1760–1823 was one of great change in the village. The remodelling of Powerscourt House from a castle to a Palladian mansion was completed around 1741 and the area became a desirable tourist destination, with the waterfall, the Dargle Valley, Lover's Leap and the Deerpark popular attractions and its 'alpine' air being prescribed for a variety of medical ailments. An early glimpse of the village in 1760 is on a map drawn of County Dublin by John Rocque.[3] Rocque was an internationally reputed cartographer who completed maps of Rome, Paris and London, and while in Ireland he had completed a map of the environs of Dublin as well as the city centre. While working on his Dublin maps, he sought aristocratic patronage here, and mapped great Irish estates including Carton and Castletown.[4] The presence of Powerscourt on his County Dublin map gives an indication of the importance of the estate and its owners. The extract containing Enniskerry village and Powerscourt is shown in Figure 1. The settlement is located at the crossing of the river, with one long street marked, aligned with the Dublin – Glendalough Road. About ten to twelve dwellings are shown, dotted around the river and along Church Hill. Powerscourt parish church was situated adjacent to house itself at the time. The ruin of this church can be seen by visitors to the estate today, east of the house near the Pepper Pot Tower.

While the new house was undoubtedly grander than the castle it replaced, several contemporary travel writers remained unimpressed. One of the earliest was Samuel Derrick, who when returning from Killarney to Dublin, made a visit to the house in 1760.[5] He mentions that there are 'many other [houses], within a mile or two, equally commodious, and infinitely more delightful'. His visit was about twenty years after the remodelling of Powerscourt House was complete. While the house was certainly impressive, the ceiling in ground floor was considered quite low for its size, and this may have discouraged some visitors from giving praise. Rocque's map would have been a useful guide for travellers and tourists to the area around this time, and there are several references to Powerscourt, Tinnehinch, the Dargle Valley, Powerscourt Waterfall, Lover's Leap and Enniskerry in contemporary travel narratives. The village is marked after the 9-mile point on the road from the city centre on the map, so it was well within a day's journey. However, while the settlement at Enniskerry was clearly established by this time, much of the travel literature in the mid-eighteenth century refers to Tinnehinch rather than Enniskerry. Arthur Young, who travelled through Ireland in 1776 and 1777 refers to 'Inniskerry' and an inn at 'Tinnyhinch' in his *Tour of Ireland*.[6] While there is a full description of Tinnehinch, and a trip to the Dargle, Enniskerry is not mentioned further, except to say that as he rode back to Dublin, he crossed 'a murmuring stream clear as crystal, and rising a hill, look[ed] back on a pleasing landscape of enclosures, which waving over hills, end in mountains of a very

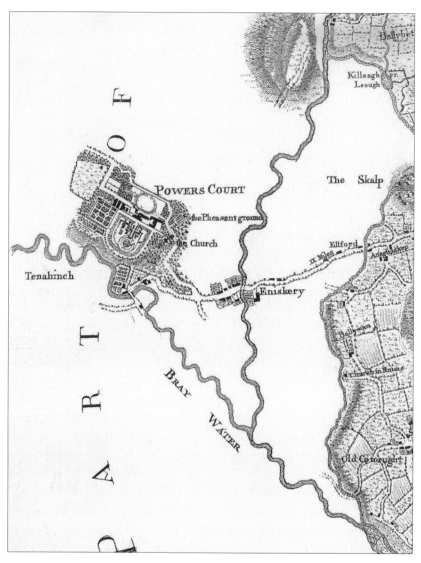

Figure 1: Extract of *An Actual Survey of the County of Dublin* by John Rocque (1760), showing Enniskerry village and Powerscourt House and Gardens. (Reproduced from a map in Trinity College Library, Dublin, with the permission of the Board of Trinity College)

Figure 2: A view of Enniskerry by A.E. McCormick, *c.* 1820. (Image reproduced courtesy of the National Library of Ireland)

noble character'. The Powerscourt Papers contain a record for the lease, dated 1780, of a house known as Tinnehinch Inn by Richard, 3rd Viscount to Isaac Delamer for three lives or thirty-one years at an annual rent of £50.[7] The inn was demolished soon after and a house for Henry Grattan built nearby, funded by a generous grant from the Irish Parliament to Grattan. A map from the Lord Monck papers of the lands around his Charleville estate show the presence of a significant building, likely to be the inn close to the junction of the Enniskerry, Kilcroney and Roundwood roads.[8]

Another traveller, Charles Topham Bowden, describes a visit to Tinnehinch and Powerscourt in 1790. His commentary described Tinnehinch, and compares Powerscourt Waterfall in a disparaging tone to others internationally, being disappointed with the flow of water.[9] There is no mention of Enniskerry in his narrative. The flow of water at Powerscourt seems to have been a common complaint; Richard Twiss, who visited Powerscourt Waterfall in 1775, considered it a poor comparison to others he had seen internationally.[10] An anonymous visitor in 1791 briefly mentions Enniskerry, but discusses in more detail dining with Grattan and his wife at Tinnehinch.[11] Enniskerry is briefly mentioned in passing in *The Traveller's Guide to Ireland*, as being on the road from Dublin to Glendalough.[12] Similarly, *The Dublin Guide* (published in 1787), describing 'the most remarkable places within a fifteen mile radius' does not mention Enniskerry, but does mention Powerscourt, the Dargle valley and even the small settlement of Delgany to the south. It is interesting to speculate therefore whether Tinnehinch would have grown into a more substantial settlement had the lands not been granted to Grattan.

As it was, Enniskerry finally came to prominence as a place of note towards the end of the eighteenth century. It is described as 'a little town belonging to Lord Powerscourt', in DeLatocnaye's *A Frenchman's Walk through Ireland in 1796–1797*.[13] He mentions an inn at Enniskerry, whose innkeeper[14] was a representative of the O'Tooles. Seward writes, in 1797 in his *Topography*, that Enniskerry is 'pleasantly situated at the foot of a hill near a river, and is of late much improved, and frequented by people for the recovery of their health'.[15]

It is evident therefore that the improvements to the village began to gather pace towards the end of the eighteenth century, perhaps coinciding with the 4th Viscountcy (1788–1809) and the 5th Viscountcy (1809–23). Richard, 4th Viscount was actively involved in Irish politics and was a prominent critic of the Act of Union. It is likely then that he took a great interest in improving his estate. In addition, the arrival of Grattan at Tinnehinch must have raised the profile of society at the village, with consequent improvements. Wright, in his book on Co. Wicklow (published in 1822), describes Enniskerry as a village with twenty-eight houses, 'scattered in an irregular and picturesque manner' and 165 inhabitants with two poor schools.[16] The 1821 census gives the total population of Powerscourt parish (village and surroundings) as 2,602.[17] Wright reported that the (late) Lord Powerscourt had recently erected a number of handsome cottages, improving the village where 'only one year since, the habitations were so wretched, that the advantage of the situation was utterly lost'. New buildings observed by Wright were the school-house and the curate's cottage. A series of buildings around this time are still present today. These include the hotel, and the buildings from the hotel along the terraces to the crossroads at the bottom of Kilgarron Hill. Also present at this time (around 1820) was the house beside the school on the north side, now Kennedy's of Enniskerry, and one large house on Church Hill, most likely Rosemount. Other buildings on Church Hill from this time include the Court House, with adjacent house on the north side, Ceres Cottage and the rectory.[18]

Complementing the information from maps and travel narratives, the work of contemporary artists provides topographical information on the nature of the area during the early history of the village. A similar trend to the travel literature is observed with topographical imagery. Mid-eighteenth century works tend to be based around Tinnehinch and the waterfall, while images of Enniskerry are not common until the beginning of the nineteenth century. By the middle of the nineteenth century, the village was very well established, and drawings of it were commonly found on maps and in travel guides. The natural beauty of the area meant that it was a popular place to paint and sketch over the course of the eighteenth and nineteenth centuries. Two of the great eighteenth-century landscape painters who visited the area during their respective tours of Ireland were Jonathon Fisher and Thomas Bates. Fisher completed a series of paintings on scenery of Ireland, including one entitled 'An Extensive View of Enniskerry' which is on display in Fota House, Cork. Despite the title, the painting is of Dargle passing through Tinnehinch, with the bridge over the river, the inn at Tinnehinch and the road towards Kilmacanogue shown. A small gate on the Powerscourt side of the river and a lodge inside this gate are also present – these were probably a precursor to the Golden Gates entrance to Powerscourt, which were positioned closer to the river after 1850, with the gates being added in 1869.[19] A painting by Thomas Bates, entitled 'A View near Enniskerry, County Wicklow', from the early 1770s is of a similar scene to Fisher's work – with the perspective hinting that it may have been drawn from the old inn itself, just opposite the old gate to Powerscourt at Tinnehinch (a small gate pillar is just visible). The painting is of the bridge crossing the Dargle, with some small houses drawn at either side.[20]

Later works from the early nineteenth century shift their focus to Enniskerry village itself and provide a contemporary picture of the developments there. McCormick sketched the village in her drawings around 1820, shown in Figure 2.[21] The drawing shows a few buildings dotted around the road from the perspective at Monastery through the village, with some houses on Church Hill visible. The Powerscourt schoolhouse is shown, as is a larger house just behind it, and a few terraces are shown opposite this, reflecting the observations made by Wright, above. Because of the perspective, the rise of the land of Knocksink prevents a view of the western end of the village. Samuel Brocas, known for his twelve views of Dublin, also compiled a series of sketches of the village, several of which are dated 15 June 1822. His view of Enniskerry Bridge is a beautiful sketch showing two small thatched houses on the village side of the river.[22] This three-arch bridge was replaced by an iron bridge, and subsequently the present elegant single-arch span around 1860. Brocas also sketched the Moss House below Lover's Leap[23] and several perspectives of Grattan's new house at Tinnehinch.[24] The village, as illustrated in these sketches from the 1820s, reaffirms Wright's description at the time; a rural, scenic place undergoing improvements for its inhabitants. Drawings incorporated in the travel literature of the 1840s show a much more developed village, consistent with today's overall structure.

Early Road Network and Pre-Ordnance Survey Place Names
Another map published in 1760 was by the cartographer Jacob Neville, shown in Figure 3. In contrast to Rocque's map, Neville's was for County Wicklow, and is full of detail with names of towns, villages, townlands, churches and other places of

significance in the locality. As well as the road from Dublin to Powerscourt identified on Rocque's map – which on Neville's map passes through 'Monastry' – additional roads are marked. The road from Enniskerry towards Annacrivey and Kilmalin is shown which subsequently goes to Glencullen – this map predates the road from Kilmalin to the military road at Glencree. The townlands noted around Enniskerry include 'Eelford', 'Barnnasiloge' 'Killmalin', 'Churchtown', 'Kilgarran' and 'Black-House'.[25] Powerscourt House and the church beside the house are both marked, as is 'Charlevile' and 'Tinnahinch'. The settlement at Enniskerry consists of a cluster of developments on the south of the river, together with more substantial dwellings, one just north of the river, and one each in Kilgarran, Monastery, Kilmalin, Ballybrew, Onagh and Stilebawn. The road from Powerscourt gate through Tinnehinch, Ballyorney and Charleville, and the road through Cookstown to Bray are also present. The latter was at the time the only road to Bray from the village, preceding the current road running along the Glencullen/Cookstown river. Jacob's nephew, Arthur Neville, produced an updated version of his map in around 1798.[26] Comparing the area around Enniskerry, the map includes similar details to the 1760 version. The houses noted in Jacob Neville's map are all present on this map, as is the mill at Enniskerry village, marked by a wheel symbol just east of the village by the river. Lord Powerscourt's Gamekeeper's Lodge, marked in 1760 west of War Hill is annotated as 'Vis. Powerscourts Old Game House' on the later map.

A notable difference between the two Neville maps for the area is the road from Kilmalin to Glencree. In the earlier map, a road is marked from Ballybrew to 'Annacrivy', stopping just before Curtlestown, with a spur to Enniskerry as indicated above. In the later map, this road is present, with a track marked from Curtlestown to the point where the river from the southern Lough Bray meets the Glencree river. In addition, the new road from 'Killmalin' through 'Clone' and 'Oldtapale' to the new military barracks at Glencree (location marked by a square symbol), and the military road itself. As the plan of the route for the military road and barracks were not finalised until the summer of 1799,[27] this would indicate that the map is from after this date, or that Neville had some information about the plans which he included on his map.

Some local information on development of the military road around Glencree can be gained from a map of the area around the proposed barracks, dated April 1799, which is in the Powerscourt Papers collection.[28] This map, commissioned by Viscount Powerscourt, shows an existing road from Rathfarnham to Glencree and the alignment of the proposed road from Glencree towards the Sally Gap at Liffeyhead (which is now the current military road south from Glencree). A road from Glencree to Enniskerry

Opposite page: Figure 3: Extracts from maps of Co. Wicklow by Jacob Neville, 1760 (top), and Arthur Neville, *c.* 1798 (bottom). (Images reproduced from maps in Trinity College Library, Dublin, with the permission of the Board of Trinity College)

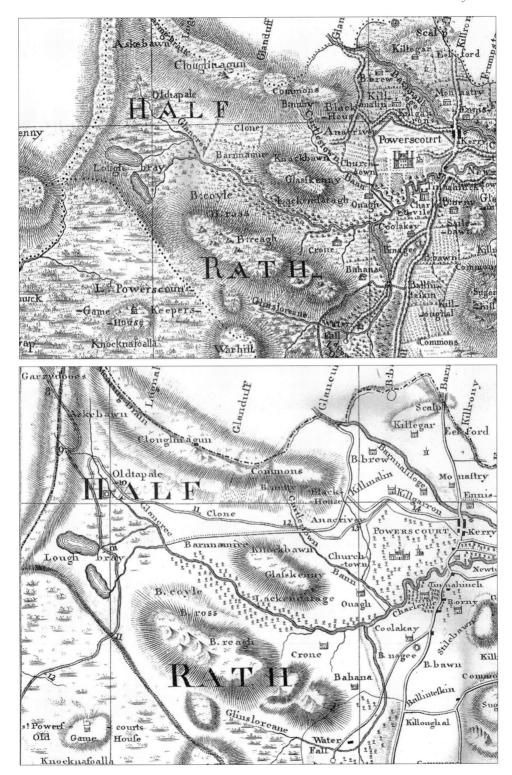

is marked, the same road marked on the earlier Neville map. This predates the current Enniskerry to Glencree road which is shown on the later Neville map. Therefore it may be that although these plans and roads predate the decision on the alignment of the military road, the plans commissioned by Powerscourt were used to influence the decision when it was ultimately made. An 1802 map attached to a lease of land[29] on which the new barracks was to be built shows the new military road, and the new Glencree to Enniskerry road (given its position north of the old road mentioned above) and several huts at Aurora. The land involved was marked on the map and was leased by Powerscourt for £3 17s 6¾d.

The Village in 1823

After the death of Richard, 5th Viscount in 1823, aged just thirty-two, his son Richard inherited the Viscountcy. However, as he was only eight years old, the estate was administered by his guardians until he came of age in 1833. From the evidence discussed above, the 4th and 5th Viscounts had done much to improve the appearance and status of the village in the period. Its layout changed from the one street format to a triangular centre, to accommodate the new road from Glencree, and terraces 'tastefully built in the cottage style'[30] are still present and recognisable today, although their appearance and form was altered during the 7th Viscount's time.[31] Two schools were built (see Chapter 2) – one in the village and one just north of the river. There were twenty-eight houses in the village in 1821. The visit of King George IV in this year, two years before the death of the 5th Viscount must have prompted a great deal of development of roads and pathways to the natural attractions in the area. These, along with houses, schools and a fever hospital (see Chapter 3), meant that Enniskerry had certainly developed a sense of place in the early part of the nineteenth century.

ONGOING DEVELOPMENT 1823–1901

With the layout of the village established by the 1820s, subsequent developments involved consolidation of community through the building of churches, establishment of graveyards and the building of the Town Clock. This period also saw the development of the great terraces at Powerscourt House as well as ambitious development plans including road building, new bridges and several attempts to build a Bray to Enniskerry railway.[32] This consolidation of community and village is demonstrated through evidence from the Ordnance Survey mapping project, Griffith's Land Valuation and documents from the Powerscourt Papers. In addition, the population and housing profile over the course of the century, described in Chapter 3, provides clues as to the movement of people during this period.

Ordnance Survey 1840

The massive Ordnance Survey project began in 1825 and involved the accurate mapping of the entire island of Ireland. The layout of the village was surveyed in 1837–8 and sketchbooks showing layout of the village as drawn by the surveyors are available to view in the National Archives.[33] The first Ordnance Survey map published in 1840 has a striking resemblance to the current layout (Figure 4). Enniskerry is at the intersection of four townlands, Monastery (213 hectares)[34] to the north, Knocksink (16.3 ha) to the west, Kilgarron (9.3 ha) to the southwest and Cookstown (121 ha) to the southeast. A small townland named Enniskerry (2.3 ha) sits to the east of the road and to the south of the river, encompassing much of what is now Millfield. In Monastery townland, an infant school house is marked just north of the river and adjacent to a dog-pound, which is situated opposite the entrance to the Bog Meadow today. A sketch by Brocas shows a view of what is likely to be the infant school, with a child outside (Figure 5).[35]

The road to Bray running along the river and the road from Enniskerry to Monastery, running by Knocksink had not been built at this stage. In Enniskerry village, (Cookstown townland), a building where the Powerscourt National School currently exists is present, although it is not marked as a school. However, given that it was a school since the early part of the century, this is likely to be an omission (it is confirmed as a schoolhouse on Griffith's survey a few years later). A post office and police station are marked in the Kilgarran townland part of the village. The fever hospital on Kilgarron Hill is present, although not annotated (again confirmed as such on Griffith's survey).[36] Two houses in Knocksink townland are identified, Grove Hill and Sea View (situated where the current Kilgarran House stands).

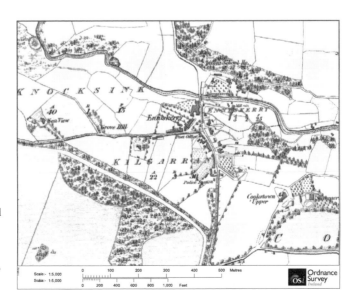

Figure 4: Ordnance Survey map of Enniskerry Village, surveyed 1837–1838, published c. 1840. Scale, 1:2500. (Map © Ordnance Survey of Ireland/ Government of Ireland – copyright permit number MP 007710)

Topographical imagery from around this time complement the Ordnance Survey map and provides a picture of the village. An image (Figure 6) produced for the book *Scenery and Antiquities of Ireland* (1842)[37] is drawn from a similar perspective to McCormick's drawing of 1820. In stark contrast to the latter, this image shows that there has been extensive development along both Church Hill and the main street in the intervening twenty years. The nature of the buildings (especially the height) should be taken in the context of the artist's perception of Sugar Loaf. A second publication, *Ireland, its Scenery and Character &c* (1841–3),[38] includes another sketch of the village (Figure 7), again from the same perspective. The bridge and hotel by the river are clearly identifiable. Both of these publications just pre-date the building of the town clock in the village in 1843.

Griffith Valuation

The Griffith Land Valuation survey, which began soon after the Ordnance Survey project, gives details of the value of all plots of land with the purpose of establishing a uniform valuation for the country. While Griffith's valuators based their own maps on the original 1840 Ordnance Survey 6 inch map, it provides more detail on the

Figure 5: Enniskerry by Samuel Brocas showing a view of Bridge at Enniskerry and building adjacent to it, which Ordnance Survey data indicates may be the infant school house. (Image reproduced courtesy of the National Library of Ireland)

Figure 6: Enniskerry from the perspective of Monastery Road, as represented in *Scenery and Antiquity of Ireland* (1842). (Image reproduced courtesy of the National Library of Ireland)

nature of the tenancies and occupiers, and being slightly later, incorporates updates to the original Ordnance Survey map. A notable difference is that the road from Church Hill running alongside the forge through Enniskerry and onto Monastery is present on Griffith's map. The development of the gardens and great terraces at Powerscourt initially began around 1842 (although they stopped in 1844 after the death of the 6th Viscount and for the duration of the minority of Mervyn, 7th Viscount) and the road along the forge may have been developed to facilitate the extra traffic and allow it to by-pass the village centre on the way to Powerscourt, or provide an easier incline to Powerscourt. There is little development reported by the valuation surveyors along this new road, but it does include a forge and yard leased to Richard Correll. The forge is dated as 1855.[39] A wooden bridge at Knocksink was built around 1855, and was replaced in 1865 by the present stone bridge.[40] Griffith also makes reference to a house just downhill from the forge, occupied by Revd Robert Daly, which is used as a house for temporary worship.[41] This of course predates the building of the new Protestant church, and indeed the Roman Catholic church at Enniskerry which are discussed in Chapter 2.

The Griffith Survey captures developments that occurred after the initial work discussed above up to 1823, and especially in the time between the building of the

Figure 7: Enniskerry from the perspective of Monastery Road, as represented in *Ireland, its Scenery and Character &c*, (1841–3). (Image reproduced courtesy of the National Library of Ireland)

Town Clock (1843) and the building of the churches (1859) (see Chapter 2). This period saw more houses on Church Hill, Ferndale, and later Lislea and Curam on the east side, Primrose Antiques, Clonlea House, the Garda Barracks on the west side. The forge, Parochial Hall, Old Rectory and two churches were built in the mid-to late 1850s. The cupola on the top of the town clock was added in 1860. Downhill from the estate office on Kilgarron Hill, four single-storey houses date from around 1840, with the additional six two-storey houses added around 1860, used to house widows. Griffith's records stated that these were 'two houses in which six widows are kept by Lord Powerscourt and the Rev Robert Daly' (whose name was later crossed out and replaced by Charles Bunall). These replaced the original Widow's House, which was uphill from the forge, opposite where the Protestant church now stands. Griffith's surveyors noted that these six houses at the bottom of Kilgarron Hill were for widows, who were named as Mrs Boyle, Mrs Stack (name subsequently crossed out and marked vacant), Mrs Dennis (name subsequently crossed out and marked vacant), Mrs Margaret Smyth, Mrs Brigid McHugh and Mrs Margaret Dempsey.[42] The architectural detail of the buildings in the village is available to view on the National Inventory of Architectural Heritage website.[43]

Just south of the river, in Enniskerry townland, a mill ruin is marked on the Ordnance Survey map. Given the date of this map, it may be that only part of the mill was a ruin. The details of the mill were surveyed around 1840. The following notes were made:[44]

Name and Description: William Williams, including a dwelling, 5 offices,[45] corn mill, kiln. Two pair of stones. One pair for wheat, inc good stone trench. The other trench but much worn 4f 6i diameter. One pair for oats much worn nearly done 4f 8i diameter. Mill wheel new 12ft diameter. Buckets 2ft 2ins wide shrouding 9ins deep, waterfall 14ft a good supply mostly all the year. Might be made an excellent mill, but at present is in very bad order. Grinds on an average six barrels each day for six months. Worth 8*s* per day Miller and Kiln man are paid 1*s* 3*d* each and the coast of coal is 1*s* 3*d* per day. £25 10*s* – yearly rent is paid for millhouse and about three Irish acres of land. Poor law valuation for all is £33 yearly. I consider it worth £40 and upwards.

Therefore it appears that the mill was in working order, albeit in poor condition. All references to the mill and buildings are removed from the Ordnance Survey 25 inch map (1888–1913), ending the long tradition of milling in the locality, which can be traced to the Powerscourt Farm Account books of 1730. A watercolour painting of a well at the mill was drawn by George Cash in 1819.[46] A sketch by Brocas of the bridge at Enniskerry[47] shows a small bridge over the mill-race on the Enniskerry side, under what is the car park at the Powerscourt Arms Hotel today (Figure 8). A portion of mill-race further downstream, east of Millfield housing estate has been

Figure 8: Extract from Enniskerry Bridge by Samuel Brocas showing the bridge and smaller bridge to the mill-race on the right-hand side. The entire structure has since been replaced. (Image reproduced courtesy of the National Library of Ireland)

preserved. A very early photograph of the village taken by Lewis Wingfield[48] shows the village around 1860 (Figure 9). The mill is present, and the old bridge drawn by Brocas and McCormick has been replaced by an iron bridge, which itself was subsequently replaced with the current bridge in the 1860s. A cutting to provide water to the mill, aligned with the mill-race in Brocas' sketch is just visible. This photograph also shows the new church in its prominent position at the top of the hill near the entrance to Powerscourt and the new houses at the bottom of Kilgarron Hill.

Local Plans

At the same time that the road from Enniskerry through Knocksink was being considered, a road from the village to Kilmolin was also being planned, with the aim of bypassing the incline at Kilgarron Hill.[49] The incline for Kilgarron Hill is given as 1 in 6½ at the steepest, whereas the new road would have had an incline at the steepest of 1 in 17. The route of the road would begin as a spur off the existing road just uphill of the fever hospital and run along Parknasilloge townland, behind where the GAA pitch is located today, meeting the present road in Kilmolin at a junction with the Glencullen Road. At this junction, 'Old Hospital – Thomas Bassett' is marked on the map. It runs through land annotated with names Tim Quigley, John Buckley, Mrs Dixon and houses marked Magee House, John Buckley's house and Edward Ward's house.[50] These surnames are present on the Griffith valuation returns. The road was never built, although the alignment does follow the existing back avenue to Kilgarron House, so some work may have been completed. The map has no date, but given that the town clock is not marked (therefore it was pre-1843) and the school in the village is present (post 1818), it seems reasonable to conclude that this map was made at a similar time to the planning of the road from Church Hill through the village and onto Knocksink. Given other developments around this time, it is likely that it was drawn between the majority of Richard, 6th Viscount (1833) and the building of the town clock (1843). The site of the 'Old Hospital' is marked in Griffith's valuation as a 'Herd's House and Land', with Benjamin Buckley as the immediate lessor. A final point to note from this map is that the hotel in the

Figure 9: Early photograph of Enniskerry taken by a member of the Wingfield family, *c.* 1860. The iron bridge and one of the mill buildings are visible to the centre-left of the picture. (Image reproduced courtesy of the National Library of Ireland)

Above & opposite Figure 10a and 10b: Photographs of Enniskerry from the Lawrence Collection, 1880–1895. (Images reproduced courtesy of the National Library of Ireland)

village is named as Miller's Hotel. This may be in reference to the presence of a mill opposite, or more likely that is run by a Miller family living in the village around this time.[51] A photograph of the village from around 1880 includes a shopfront with the sign T.B. Millers over the door.

Another map (dated 1834) of similar format and scale outlines plans for realignment of the road from near the entrance gate to Powerscourt Waterfall and running towards Bahana.[52] On the 1840 Ordnance Survey map, the road from the waterfall entrance passes over a wooden bridge. The bridge is marked as a footbridge on the plans for the new road. The road, which was subsequently built and follows the existing alignment, involved construction of a new bridge, '18 feet wide and about 60 feet long'.[53] It is not clear whether it was built at this time and replaced, or was not built at all until 1847, as the Powerscourt papers show designs[54] by John Louch, the estate architect, for two bridges – one labelled 'Bridge near Waterfall'. In any case, the bridge served well until 1986, when it was destroyed by Hurricane Charlie. The second of the two bridges drawn by Louch is entitled 'Bridge on double stream on upper part of new road'. No more details are given, but its design matches exactly that of the impressive bridge that was eventually built at Knocksink in 1865.

Mervyn, 7th Viscount recounts that a team of workers under the guidance of Tom Parnell, uncle of Charles Stuart Parnell, built several roads around the parish during the years of the famine:[55]

> Tom Parnell … was a poor man who was employed to lay out various roads and drives etc … take charge of a gang of labourers, who were to carry out his directions, and as the time was the years 1846, 1847 and 1848, when Ireland was in a very distressed state on account of the potato Famine, it was considered that the best manner to combat the distress was to employ the poor in useful works. My guardians accordingly used their powers in giving employment to all the poor tenants on the estate, and also improved the estate by the works which they instituted, and which were carried out by them.

Roads built by these men include the road in Deerpark, from the entrance gate below up to the paddock gate, called 'The Lady's Drive', after Mervyn, 7th Viscount's mother; and the road descending from the paddock back to the waterfall with many turns and curves, 'The Earl's Drive'. Parnell also laid out the Tinnehinch Avenue, where 'there was formerly only a steep breakneck road down to the river from the house'.

Powerscourt estate workmen's account books around the period 1855 make several references to workmen been assigned to work on the Tinnehinch road.[56]

One important road that was built after the original Ordnance Survey was recorded was the Enniskerry to Bray road following the river – the lower Cookstown 'Twenty-One Bends' road. Before this road was built, the upper Cookstown road was the main route to Bray. The advantage of the lower road was that it was flat, although obviously took a lot of work to cut the road out from the bank. Sphagnum rock dug out from this road was used in the construction of the gardens at Powerscourt in the 1860s, and can be seen where where the boathouse and the the Japanese gardens are today.[57]

The Village at the End of the Century

After boom in building in the village during the short lifetime of the 6th Viscount and the early years of the 7th Viscount, the pace of development slowed towards the end of the century. In the years after the Famine, Ireland enjoyed something of a boom, and Powerscourt would have enjoyed good incomes from increased rents from tenants who could afford to pay them.[58] By the end of the 1870s this boom was over, and consequently development in the village slowed. Nevertheless, the combination of road networks and developments in the village meant that Enniskerry had become a very accessible and extremely attractive village. The Ordnance Survey map of 1883 encompasses all of the developments discussed above. The road network is greatly improved, with the lower Cookstown road and the road through Knocksink to Monastery present, along with two stone bridges at Enniskerry and Knocksink. There is a consolidation of the buildings along Church Hill, along with the new houses, noted by Griffith, at the bottom of Kilgarron Hill. The village obtained a second school, on the site of the current library and of course gained two fine churches (see Chapter 2). In terms of overall structure, this map differs little from the village today.

Photographs from the village around 1880–1890 are available from the Lawrence Collection at the National Library. Two perspectives are shown in Figure 10. The first shows a view from Church Hill towards the north. The frontage of the Powerscourt Arms Hotel differs from the modern-day equivalent. The hotel is one of the oldest buildings in the village, and is most likely the inn mentioned by DeLatocnaye in 1797. It was remodelled around 1835 but destroyed by a fire in December 1894. A newspaper article at the time reported that:[59]

> Mrs Frank Buckley, wife of the proprietor, stated that at about twenty minutes to four she heard a crackling noise, and told her husband that something was burning. On going down the stairs, Mr Buckley found the place full of smoke and the bar and pantry on fire … in removing one of Mr Buckley's young children, Miss Norman, telegraph clerk at the local Post office, mistook one of the passages and turned towards the fire. Fortunately Mr Buckley was close at hand and rescued the young lady and child … Mr Michael Wogan,

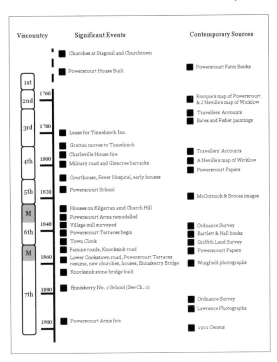

Viscountcy		Significant Events	Contemporary Sources

Figure 11: Indicative timeline of significant developments and important sources of contemporary information on the development of the village (some manuscript sources omitted for clarity). 'M' indicates a period of minority in the Viscountcy, when the estate was monitored by guardians.

junior, rendered excellent service by cutting the main building away from the range of out offices which connected the premises to the other houses on the western side of the village.

The hotel was subsequently rebuilt, modelled on the previous style, with some extra gables on the front. A photograph taken from the same perspective just after the rebuilding of the hotel is available to view in the National Photographic Archive (Album 45). Advertisements for the new hotel were placed in *The Irish Times* on 2 May 1896.

The second image is a view from the village southwards up Church Hill. The spire of the new church is present. The inn has the name Leicester Arms. The 7th Viscount was married to Lady Julia Coke, daughter of the 2nd Earl of Leicester. Her bust can be seen in the gardens at Powerscourt. To one side of the Leicester Arms is T.B. Millers. As mentioned above, there were earlier references to Millers in the village, although there are none listed in the 1901 Census. To the other side of the Leicester Arms is Livery Stables. Several other images of the village are available in the National Library's collection.

SUMMARY

The development of the village of Enniskerry up to 1901 can be considered over three main periods – establishment, development and continuance. The period of establishment of a settlement coincided with and followed on from the building of Powerscourt House, and saw a small rural community develop around the bridge at Enniskerry. The period of development of the settlement and community coincided with the visit of George IV, the peak in population of the parish and the subsequent majority of the 6th Viscount – a golden age in the development of the village – culminating in the 7th Viscount's majority and the building of two churches in the village. Finally, the period of continuance of the settlement, over the remainder of the century from early 1860s, coinciding with the 7th Viscount's life at Powerscourt, which saw the number of people working on the land decline and the village at Enniskerry settle into a way of life that remained relatively unchanged over the course of this period. In the next part of the book, the lives of the people during the latter two periods will be examined in more detail, through a consideration of two major influences during the nineteenth century – education and religion.

2

EDUCATION AND RELIGION

Education 1825–1835 – Local Tensions: Setting the Scene for the National School System – Board of National Education 1831–1901 – Impact of Education on the Populace – Religion – The Reformatory at Glencree – Summary

This chapter tracks the development of education provision in the village, from the arrangements before the Board of Education came into place in 1831 and the subsequent establishment and local implementation of the National School system, initially at Curtlestown. The education of the village's youth was dominated by the underlying context of faith, despite the Board of Education's efforts to the contrary. The efforts of both denominations to win the minds and souls of the village's youth are discussed, along with the development of the religious communities in the village over the course of the nineteenth century. Finally, at the edge of the parish, the Glencree Reformatory was established in 1859, and its role in education is presented.

EDUCATION 1825–1835

In 1825, the Commission of Irish Education Enquiry published their second report, which included a nationwide survey of schools in the country at that time, revealing the large extent of pay schools and voluntary provision of education that existed. The table for Powerscourt parish is reproduced in Table 2.[1] The information gathered included the name of the head teacher and their religion, whether the school was a pay school, the total income of the head teacher, a description of the building, the number of pupils in the school, according to both Established Church (Protestant) and Roman

Townland	Name of Master/Mistress	Religion of Master/Mistress	Free or Pay	Total Annual Income of Master/Mistress	Description of the School house and Probable Cost thereof	Number of Pupils in Attendance on an average of Three Months preceding this return								Societies, Associations, &c with which the schools are connected, or whether assisted by local patronage and in what manner, stating such as Parish Schools	Scriptures whether read or not in the school
						By the Protestant Return				By the Roman Catholic Return					
						Prote stant	R. C.	M	F	Prote stant	R. C.	M	F		
Annacrony	John Cranston	Protestant	Pay	60 *l*	Lime and stone: cost from 400 *l* to 500 *l*; half the expense defrayed by the rector, the remainder by the parish	72	25	74	23	88	20	78	30	Parish school. Assoc. For discountenancing vice. The Rev. R. Daley, pays the master 15*l* per annum	Read; A.V.
Charleville	Mrs. Hall	Protestant	Pay	32 *l* 10 *s*	Built of stone and lime, cost 200 *l*	49	26	40	35	29	22	38	33	The Earl and Countess of Rathdown pay the mistress 12 *l* 10*s* p.a. The Earl of Rathdown built the schoolhouse.	Read; A.V.
BushyP'arle [sic]	Henrietta Farrell	Protestant	Free	20 guineas	Built of lime and stone by Col. Howard for about 100 *l*	13	3	–	16	16	3	–	19	Hon. H. Howard built the schoolhouse and pays the master's salary	Read; A.V.
Ballywaltrim	Mrs. Ormsby— Rev. J. Shields classical teacher	Protestant	Pay	Each pupil pays 80 guineas p.a.	Built of the best materials, cost about 200*l*	8		8		12			12	None	Read; A.V.
Cookstown	John Murray	Protestant	Pay	36*l* 14*s*	Circular room, 24 ft in diameter	19	7	20	6	–	–	–	–	Lord Powerscourt pays ___ *s*; the rector d' 21 to the master	Read; A.V.
Cookstown	Margaret Sandford	Protestant	Pay	35*l* 12*s* 9*d*	Consists of four rooms, 600*l*	25	36	14	47	–	–	–	–	Lord Powerscourt pays 34*l* 10*s* to the mistress, and built the schoolhouse	Read; A.V.
Annacroney	Anne Pearce	Protestant	Pay	Children pay 3s per q'.	A cabin built of stone and mud	3	8	4	7	3	8	4	7	None	Read; B.V.
Ballenleskin	Anne Wilmot	R. C.	Pay	Pupils pay 2/2 per q'.	A bad cabin	–	6	1	5	–	–	–	–	None	Read; D.V.
Old Bally	Eleanor Maher	R. C.	Pay	About 13*l*	A wretched cabin without a window	10	21	15	16	10	20	10	20	The rector pays for 14 children at 2*s* 2*d* per quarter	Read; B.V.
Clune	Bernard McMahon	R. C.	Pay	Pupils pay from 2*d* to 3*d* per week	The end of an old turf house, without door, window or chimney	2	18	9	11	–	–	–	–	None	Read; D.V.
Enniskerry	Hannah Buckley	Protestant	–	Not stated	Built of lime and stone; cost about 115*l*	–	–	–	–	20	15	10	25	Lady Powerscourt and the protestant curate	Read; Estab. V.

Catholic Church returns and whether the school was supported by any of the several education societies that existed at the time. The data demonstrates that there were several schools scattered about the parish. Lord and Lady Powerscourt sponsored three schools in or near the village; a school in Enniskerry village and two in Cookstown. The Protestant rector, Revd Daly, sponsored one at 'Annacrony', which is likely to be Annacrivey as well as supporting one of the schools at Cookstown (Enniskerry) and a second school in the village. Between them, these schools registered between 136 to 152 Protestant children and 78 to 83 Roman Catholic children, depending on the returns used. Both Established Church and Roman Catholic returns were requested as each community had an interest in the numbers reported. The Established Church wished to demonstrate that the education system in place sufficiently met the needs of both Protestant and Roman Catholic children, while the Roman Catholic Church wanted children of their faith educated independently by Catholic teachers.

Unfortunately this debate was to linger over the education system for the remainder of the century. Problems with the system are obvious in examining the returns. For example, considering the returns for three rural schools at Ballenleskin, Old Bally (Old Boleys) and Clune, the buildings were described as 'a bad cabin', 'a wretched cabin without a window' and 'the end of an old turf house, without door, window or chimney' respectively. One of these was supported by the rector. In evidence to the commission in 1824, the Protestant rector Revd Daly states that he supports a school, taught by a Roman Catholic woman, not qualified so well as a Protestant master/mistress, but well-conducted and of good character. The school is 'in the wildest part of the mountains, about five miles [from Enniskerry]'. He also says that there are hedge schools, 'where they teach Roman Catholic catechism, but they are very bad schools indeed'.[2]

The returns for all eleven schools in the parish total to 221 Protestant and 165 Roman Catholic children, based on the Protestant returns (using Catholic numbers for the school in Enniskerry which had no returns from Protestant clergy) or 224 Protestant children and 154 Roman Catholic children based on the Catholic returns (again filling gaps using Protestant numbers). These totals (386 and 378 respectively) far exceed the 1821 census, which reports that there were 181 pupils in the village. The census also states that Revd Robert Daly pays for about forty pupils in one school and fourteen in another.

Ten years after the Commissioners of Irish Education Inquiry published their report, a subsequent report on the state of public instruction in Ireland was published. The Commissioners of Public Instruction were required to determine the means of education in each parish, detailing the schools average attendance, whether this has been increasing or decreasing and the sources of funding. The report provides

Opposite page: *Table 2: Details of schools in the Diocese of Dublin, Parish of Powerscourt as reported by the Commissioners of Irish Education Enquiry, 1825.*[3, 4]

information on Powerscourt schools under the old parish name Stagonil.[5] It lists ten schools, consisting of seven daily schools, an infant school and two Sunday schools. The description of all except the Sunday schools gives the master's or mistress' name instead of location, so a direct comparison with the 1825 report, above, is not possible. However, in the case of Annacrivey School, the master's name is again listed as Cranston, with an average daily attendance of seventy, a number which has remained unchanged over the previous five years. It does not state whether they were supported by an education societies (as they were in 1825). The Protestant rector, stated in a response to a question on the matter of support of education societies in the 1825 Enquiry that there was only one school supported by such a society in his parish.[6] The rector also supports the Annacroney school kept by Cranston, which has ninety pupils on the books. Lord Powerscourt is named as supporter of two schools, one kept by James Moore and one kept by John Murray. The former has an average daily attendance of forty-eight (and increasing), and the latter twenty or twenty-one. One of these is likely to be the school in Enniskerry village, the other a school in Cookstown. Lady Powerscourt supported a daily school kept by Miss Tunstall, with nine boys and twenty-three girls on the books and an infant school, kept by Miss Price, which had fifteen boys and twenty-four girls on the books. All of the listed daily schools state they have reading, writing, arithmetic and scriptural instruction (and in the case of Miss Tunstall's class, needlework for girls). The final day school is kept by William Cosgrave (stated as being a teacher there since May 1834, and implied that he is responsible for the increasing attendance), which does not state scriptural instruction in its subjects. It is housed in a schoolroom provided by Roman Catholic ministers, and scholars pay 2*s* 6*d* to 5*s* quarterly. This is most likely to be the school at Curtlestown, which applied for National School status on 9 July 1834, and was taken in by the Commissioners for National School Education within a year. The Commission had strict rules about the separation of school and religious instruction, and if such instruction was being taught in 1834, it is probable that the school did not wish to report it given it had just submitted an application to the board. A Sunday school is held at Powerscourt gate, attended by 190 or 200 pupils, and a 'Charlemont Sunday School' is also listed. Interestingly, none of the schools listed are hedge schools. It may be that the school at Curtlestown replaced the three Roman Catholic school gatherings listed in 1825, although the details for Curtlestown in the National School documents state that it was present at the current site since 1818. Nevertheless, in the intervening ten years, the facility for education of Catholic children had improved. The imminent incorporation of Curtlestown into the National School system would ensure that the school existed under a stable and regulated system.

LOCAL TENSIONS: SETTING THE SCENE FOR THE NATIONAL SCHOOL SYSTEM

By the time the National School Board was established in 1831, there had been several Parliamentary inquiries into the state of the education system, or lack of, in Ireland, including the 1825 Irish Education Enquiry described above, and the Commissioners for the Board of Education (1806–1812) which was critical of the current system and recommended changes which were essential, and would eventually become incorporated into the National School Board.[7] The education system in Ireland was influenced and supported by religious education societies and local benefactors with proselytism and allegations of proselytism rife. The extent to which this was a problem in Enniskerry is captured in the 1825 Commissioners Enquiry, which held interviews, on oath, with both the Protestant rector of the parish, Revd Robert Daly, and the parish priest of Bray (which included responsibility for Enniskerry at the time), Revd James Doyle. Revd Doyle's curate in Enniskerry was also called Revd Daly. James Doyle was interviewed on 16 December and Robert Daly interviewed on the 15 December 1824.

The protestant clergyman Robert Daly was asked in his interview about the attendance at his schools and the nature of the instruction. He states that there are five schools established by private funds in the parish, and one supported by the Association for Discountenancing Vice (a Protestant education society), and that children attend these schools 'with great anxiety,[8] except as far as they are prohibited by the Roman Catholic clergymen'. When asked whether the schools could accommodate more children he states:[9]

> Yes; but we would build more if the children would come; we could educate them to any amount. I should say that within a short time the Revd Mr Doyle, Roman Catholic rector had an interview with myself, and some of the leading persons concerned in education, and he has consented to the children going to the schools upon the system of the Kildare-place institution, and we have agreed that there should be no comment of any kind upon the scriptures in the every day schools; but the other priest, Revd Mr Daly, I understand says he will not allow any children to go to schools where the scriptures are read; he told me so himself last year, and I do not believe he has withdrawn his opposition since the Roman Catholic rector agreed with us that he would admit the schools upon that system.

The Kildare Place Society was founded in 1811, and its mission was 'to afford the same advantages of education to all classes of professing Christians, without interfering with the peculiar religious opinions of any'. The Society model (and subsequently the National School model which replaced it) allowed for the Bible to be read in class, once there was no comment on it.[10] The Roman Catholic curate in Enniskerry, Revd Daly, objected to the reading of the New Testament at all, according to his parish priest, and probably objected to the presence of a Protestant master, which was to be a recurring problem for the Roman Catholic clergy for the remainder of the century. While this agreement between Doyle and Robert Daly related to a specific school supported by Lady Rathdowne at Charleville, Robert Daly was a supporter of the Kildare Place Society and its principles generally. The problem appeared to have been somewhat historical in the parish, with a block to progress arising from a dispute between the newly arrived parish priest in Bray and his curate at Enniskerry. The latter was, according to Robert Daly's evidence, been in the village for seven or eight years (c. 1816–1817).

The parish priest in Bray, James Doyle, in his evidence on the topic, stated that upon preparing for his contribution to the Commission, he discovered that Lady Rathdowne's school was 'exceeding very much' the principles of the Kildare Place Society in her school, and that through mediation with Revd Daly, Lady Rathdowne would in future conform to these principles in her daily school, but not the Sunday school.[11] When asked why he didn't just remove the Roman Catholic children from the school, he stated:[12]

Because I look on education as necessary for the poor in particular, and the nation in general; and it is not only more becoming in me, as a minister of religion, but more useful to my flock; and in a national point of view, still more useful to accommodate the matter, if possible.

He admitted that this would not be the general view of Roman Catholic clergymen. After the new arrangements were in place, he said that he would communicate them to the parish in parishioners in Powerscourt and 'shall not only allow, but encourage' them to go to this school.

It would appear from this that both clergymen were moderate in their views, although later evidence demonstrated that despite Revd James Doyle's willingness to encourage students attendance at schools run on this model, he had a mistrust of the sincerity of the motives of the Kildare Place Society. As discussed, his view on Roman Catholic children attending schools modelled on Kildare Place was not shared by his curate in Enniskerry, Revd Daly. Doyle told the commissioners that his curate is 'far removed from me and is not so much under my control' and that 'my predecessor gave him that district for his exclusive management'. Revd Robert Daly stated that the problems with schools in the parish arose with the curate's arrival five or six years ago – before that there was a priest 'not very clerical in his character', who did not interfere. Tracing the withdrawal of Roman Catholic children from the schools, he states that when he first set up a school (from the context it would seem he is referring to the school at Annacrivey) the majority were Roman Catholic children, but that by degrees, they have become a minority (26 out of 114 on the roll) in November 1824. In discussing the means by which children were removed, he states:[13]

> … when they first began, they began quietly; they used to take the children to their stations and then they quietly removed them without any noise; they succeeded more in that way than when they began to speak out plainly against the Scripture education; then the people began to rebel, and said they would send their children …
>
> I have gone to many houses, and seen seven or eight children training up in total ignorance; and the people said it was the priest who forbade them to send them to school; in my parish where they have prohibited them from going to our schools, they have provided no others … but lately they are building a school near the chapel in my parish; but till now, all their efforts to keep the children from our schools, were unaccompanied with providing any other schools for them; there are only 150 children going to schools out of 2400 Roman Catholics, while there are 197 going out of 800 Protestants.

In response to a query on whether he thought the new school would aid the withdrawal of Roman Catholic children from his school, he replied that he thought it would for a while, but that 'people generally think they are not so well taught in their schools as ours'.

There is no evidence to say whether Doyle's position did indeed result in uptake of education, later priests in the parish objected repeatedly to schools with a Protestant management joining the National School system, on the basis that they would have Protestant masters. While this argument reflected one that was going on in parishes around the country, it had of course real effects on the lives of the people. Roman Catholic parents, keen to educate their children were caught between balancing the desire to send their children to school and not wanting to incur the wrath of local clergymen. There are several strands to the 'encouragement' of attending a school or not, depending on the side reporting. These included allegations of the threat of eviction and inducements to attend school from the Roman Catholic side and allegations of being threatened with removal from the Church on the Protestant side.

James Doyle, in his testimony stated that one parishioner he spoke to had eight children, and was living on Lord Rathdowne's land. The parishioner was convinced that he would be dismissed if he did not send his children, and therefore was sending them under duress. This parishioner would instruct the children according to his Christian doctrines in the evening, so that 'the impressions they might receive elsewhere … had no fear of remaining on the children's minds'. Challenged by the Inquiry that this parishioner was merely making this case so as to make an excuse for what was actually a free choice, the priest said he thought he was sincere. He said that while he knew of no cases of eviction or threatened eviction in his twelve months in the parish, a child had told him that he heard Lady Rathdowne say as much, and in addition he had heard his curate, Mr Daly, state frequently that parishioners were threatened with dismissal. Revd Robert Daly, in his testimony, dismisses any allegation that landlords might exert their authority to influence their tenantry to attend schools objected to by their priests. He stated that he said it to Lord Powerscourt that it was a 'singular thing that not one Roman Catholic child that lived in [his] demesne attended Sunday Schools; and I asked him if he would not speak to them'. Revd Daly stated that Lord Powerscourt's reply was that if the parents refused to send their children to Sunday school, he would not request them to do so.

Allegations of inducements were also a feature of the Inquiry. James Doyle in his testimony stated that Lady Rathdowne had acknowledged the use of rewards and premiums, including clothing, although it is open to interpretation as to whether these were for 'good answering' or merely for attendance. One can imagine that if such inducements did exist, even for good answering, that it would be an attractive reason to attend the school.

Fear of the Roman Catholic clergymen was another factor in the debate. Revd Robert Daly, in his submission stated that one family:

> of the name of Norris, and they went three times to their duty, as they call it, when the priest held a station in the neighbourhood, and they were three times sent away; the man, as I am informed, told both priests he would rather cut off his hands that take the children away from the schools, for in truth they had no other schools to but those, and the people are fond of schools.

He recounts another tale of meeting a man and his two children at their house 'up the long hill where he lives' and says that the children there were removed from the school six weeks ago. The father explained that he thought it was the worst thing to have to remove his children from the school, but they had to give themselves up to the priest entirely. As they were talking, the priest suddenly appeared on the horizon, Daly left, 'lest I should bring upon him the priest's anger'. This just preceded Revd Doyle's permission to attend the every-day school again, and Daly said that the children had come to both the day and Sunday schools – he was not sure if it was confusion over the nature of the permission or a willingness to attend both schools regardless. The priest also forbade children in attending an infant school at Enniskerry, which catered for four to six year olds. To ensure high numbers, a caravan was sent 2 miles up into the mountains every day bringing twenty or thirty children, who were provided with a meal by Lady Powerscourt every day. Revd Robert Daly, said that the priest, Revd Daly objected to Roman Catholic children attending saying that 'it was the greatest attempt that was ever made to make heretics of them from their very youth'. There were no Roman Catholic children in the school.

While Revd James Doyle's permission may have eased the tension somewhat for the daily schools, there is evidence throughout the interviews that the argument over Sunday school attendance was a continuance of what had occurred in the daily schools. One is struck by a sense of helplessness of the community trying to educate their children, caught in the middle of a turf war for the minds and souls of the parish's youth.

BOARD OF NATIONAL EDUCATION 1831–1901

In 1831 the Board of National Education was established, with an annual grant of £30,000 formerly provided to the Kildare Place Society. The purpose of the Board was to support non-denominational schools, with separate secular, religious and moral instruction, designed to prevent proselytism. Religious instruction was allowed only if it took place at a fixed hour and children could be exempt if their parents so wished. The Board controlled the books used, and eventually published their own lesson books which were given in either free-stock or at reduced prices. An inspectorate would ensure rules of the system were adhered to. Initially applications for aid required signatures from both Protestant and Roman Catholic communities, but this was later relaxed to just requiring a reporting of the opinion of the other community in applications.[14]

Curtlestown National School
Of all the schools existing in Enniskerry, initially only Curtlestown applied to be 'taken into connexion with the Board', with its initial application being submitted on 9 July 1834, and was officially recognised as a National School on 9 July 1835. Given roll number 1119 and entered into the minute books as 'Cuttlestown' (the 'r' in the original application looks like a 't', so in a beautiful demonstration of bureaucracy, it remained as Cuttlestown for at least the remainder of the century!)

The initial application[15] was for a 'Fitting-Up' of the school, since the school house was already built. It stated that the school was established in 1818, although this may refer to a gathering at this site, as we know from the 1825 reports that it was being built at this time. The school house was built by local subscription of stone and lime, with a slated roof and was 37½ft by 13ft. There was one school room, with sixteen seats, 70ft of desks sufficient to accommodate 150 children. In keeping with the principles of the Board, the school would in future restrict religious instruction to Saturdays. Students paid what they can afford, but about forty were free. The teacher was William Cosgrave (as named in the 1835 Irish Education Inquiry) and the application is for a salary for him. A note at the back approves a salary of £10 per annum from 1 April (presumably 1835). The correspondent was Revd Patrick Black, curate. The applications at this time required the support of both communities. The signatures under the Protestant heading are Mrs Grattan, Rich Burton, William Quigley, Wingfield Burtton, Joseph Burton, Timothy Quigley, Abraham Williams and [unreadable] Evans. The signatures under the Roman Catholic heading are [unreadable] Roche P.P., Patrick Black C.C, L. Fitzsimon, Thaddeus [unreadable] Gray, Seamus Dixon, M Callagherry, John Mcannsey and Bryan Ryder. The entire application is transcribed in the Appendix.

Because the system was centrally administered, a good set of records exists on the management of each school. The minute register books for Curtlestown can be used to trace its history over the remainder of the century.[16, 17, 18, 19] The table below shows the teachers employed over the period 1835–1901, along with any comments on them that arise out of the minute books and points of note from various applications for support. The school had one teacher until 1855, when it also appointed a workmistress. The arrival of Michael Cunningham in 1863 coincided with the establishment of an evening school, which he was to tutor. Given that he was just nineteen, and that the average age of the boys attending the evening school was also nineteen, this cannot have been an easy task, but one he appears to have carried out well enough to warrant praise.

The report on the application for support of an evening school stated that he was competent, and his method of conducting the school was attentive and wholly efficient.

Teacher	Comments
William Cosgrave	Appointed at time of association with board, with salary of £10 per annum to be paid from 1 April 1835.
William Byrne	Appointed 11 October 1836.
John Byrne	Appointed 14 April 1837, retired 21 May 1861. Towards the end of his career, John Byrne was repeatedly receiving bad comments in the minute book. He was admonished in May 1855 for 'low proficiency of pupils and for want of application and earnestness in the discharge of his duties generally', and again in August 1858 'on the low profession of pupils'. In November 1860, he was reprimanded 'severely on the discreditable state of classes for the state of which in a literary point of view, he is for the future to be entirely responsible'. A note on 8 February 1861 states that a retiring allowance of thirty months salary will be awarded, on condition that he finally retire from office of public instructor by 21 May 1861, leaving school records and free stock in a satisfactory condition. A note on 30 August states that some material was removed by Mr Byrne, but that inspector subsequently

reported that they were purchased by Mr Byrne and that no further action would be taken.

Margaret Dowling	Appointed May 1855 and left June 1893. During her long career as workmistress in the school, she had a difficult relationship with the inspectors. She was temporarily recognised as an assistant, but was sacked from this position and reinstated as a workmistress. In addition, her salary for her position as workmistress was removed at times due to low average attendance in the school. One good comment for her in the minute books is that in 1855, soon after her appointment, Marchioness Londonderry, present during an inspection, reported she 'was much pleased with the needlework'.
Michael Cunningham	Appointed July 1861, aged nineteen. An additional £5 salary was provided to give evening instruction in January 1862. In September 1862, he was cautioned to 'exert himself more zealously for the involvement of his school and pay due attention to the instructions of the inspector.' A similar note regarding the instructions of the inspector was issued in September 1863.
Anne Toole	Appointed September 1863 as senior monitress of fourth year. Her application in July 1863 states she was sixteen years old. Her qualifications 'do not at present warrant her appointment as an assistant'. She was admonished in September 1864 for 'low answering', and would be dismissed again if so unprepared.
Michael McGuinness	Appointed as an assistant from 1 November 1865, with salary of £15. This was on a trial basis, on condition that the attendance would increase and that McGuinness would teach in the evening school. On 30 April 1866, the school manager was informed that the salary would not be continued since the attendance was insufficient.
Evan Phillips	27 November 1866, admonished on accounts. In 1871, admonished for smoking in the schoolroom, for non-observance of the timetable. More attention was to be

given to writing from dictation and grammar, and the reading and geography of 3rd class. Salary withdrawn from May 1873, and a retirement gratuity of £142 7s 6d awarded to him.

Cath Conlan	Appointed Senior Monitress from 1 May 1868. Attention called to her 'insufficient answering' in March 1870.
Bridget Doogan	Appointed Senior Monitress July 1870. Dismissed March 1873 for insufficient answering at examinations. Manager's application to have her reinstated refused as her answering at the last examination was 'in the highest degree unsatisfactory'.
Sarah Morrin	Appointed as an assistant from March 1875.
Jeremiah Golden	Listed as the principal in an application for Sarah Morrin in 1875. In January 1876 admonished on sale stock to be provided, out offices to be cleaned and repaired. To give ¾ hour extra instruction to monitor. (Jeremiah Golden was subsequently the master at Enniskerry No. 2 NS)
J. Dolan	Appointed November 1875. In November 1877, a note refers to a charge of drunkenness and disorderly conduct against him, saying the explanation is accepted and he is to be cautioned to be more guarded in the future. Left January 1878.
J. Costello	Named as principal, January 1878. In 1880, he was dismissed from May 1880, but subsequently remained on trial. In August 1880, cautioned as to rolls not being called. Dismissed again in September 1881 for low answering.
Mary J. Dempsey	Appointed principal during temporary dismissal of J. Costello, and again until she left August 1891.
C O'Rourke	Appointed principal September 1891. Mrs Alicia O'Rourke was workmistress from September 1893 and subsequently appointed assistant from April 1901.

The evening school pupils were all male, with an average age nineteen. There were employed in various occupations – twelve as turf-cutters, the remainder (of twenty-three) were farm labourers or farmer's sons. The inspector's comment on the report concluded that:[20]

> The education of young men in the locality has been much neglected owing to the demand for field labour, and the disposition for improvement which the [unreadable] shown deserves to be encouraged. This disposition deems to have sprung up with a sudden impulse but the lesson of this apparently precipitate and unusual desire for instructions seems to be that a fair teacher has only recently got charge of this school. Whether these young men will persevere or not is uncertain but the experiment of giving a grant to aid them seems worth trying.

Other references to improvements in attendance due to a change in teaching staff are implied in other reports. In an application for aid to fund Anne Toole's salary in 1863, the local inspector reports that the average in the year previous has jumped from thirty-six males and thirty-five females to sixty-six males and sixty females, attributed to the presence of a teacher in whom the public have confidence replacing an 'inefficient teacher'.[21] It would appear from the data that teacher in whom the public have confidence is Cunningham, who replaced John Byrne.

A similar note is attached to the report on an application for aid towards the salary of an assistant teacher. It states that the attendance has increased hugely since the superannuation of E. Phillips.[22] It is difficult to know the true cause of this increase, as it coincided with a time when the National School at Enniskerry was closed (see below). At the end of the century, the principal Christopher O'Rourke is listed on the 1901 Census, living in Curtlestown Lower, aged thirty-four, which means he was twenty-four at the time of his appointment. His wife was thirty in 1901. Both state they are National School teachers. According to the 1911 census, they are living in Enniskerry village, and are again both listed as teachers. Curtlestown National School relocated from its original position by the church to a new site nearby in the 1960s. The original schoolhouse is now a private residence.

Enniskerry National School (Powerscourt)

Powerscourt applied for association with the National Board and became connected in January 1867. This may have been precipitated by the retirement of John Cranston, who having been at Annacrivey, had moved to the school in the village by the mid-1840s. His name, along with other teachers paid by Powerscourt, appear on the servant's wages account for 1844.[23] Cranston received £40 per annum, with Ellen Tanner, school mistress at Enniskerry, receiving £30. The wages also include a salary for Philip O'Connor at Annacrivey (£30) and John Parker at Glencree (£25). Other archives from the Powerscourt Papers related to Cranston at Enniskerry include his signatures on a wide variety of expense receipts attributed to the school in 1846.

These include a receipt for payment to Patrick Byrne for work done in the Cranston's garden at the schoolhouse (7s), payment to John Byrne for carpentry work completed at the school (10s), payment to William Sullivan for repairing clocks at the school (7s 6d), annual payment to Myles Byrne for cleaning privies at the infant school and the main school (15s) and payment to Mary Magrane for cleaning schools (15s per quarter).[24] The latter includes a note from Cranston saying that Mary Magrane's work had been much better than before. If Cranston was a schoolmaster at Annacrivey at the time of the Irish Education Inquiry in 1825, it is feasible that he could have retired in the 1860s, which may have led to the application for the school to be taken into connection with the National School system.

On the original application, James Doherty, aged thirty and his wife Isabella, aged twenty-four are listed as schoolmaster and mistress. James received training from the Church Education Society. The school building was described in the application as being 44ft long and 16ft wide, with six large windows. A portion of the house was occupied by the teacher, with 'no inconvenience to the school'. The average attendance was twenty, with twenty-seven males and eleven females on the books. In applying, Lord Powerscourt, through his agent Mr Posnett, undertook to carry out any improvements requested by the Board. The inspector had an interview with the Roman Catholic priest, Revd Mr O'Dwyer. In a reflection of previous times, he objected to the school because of the presence of a Protestant teacher, and would 'oppose the attendance of any children of his flock while such teachers are employed there'. A salary of £15 was approved for Mr Doherty.[25] The school was given the roll number 9760.

The minute books again provide some insight into the running of the school.[26, 27, 28] Viscount Powerscourt was listed as the patron and Revd Charles McDonagh was the correspondent. The teacher was James Doherty, who was appointed in December 1866, and who left in January 1871. He was succeeded by Denis A. Christian, who left in April 1875. Mr Christian was admonished and threatened with a fine in 1874, and was reprimanded again in 1875 for irregularities in school accounts. Replying to a query from the manager (at this time Revd H. Galbraith), the commissioners considered Mr Christian's conduct worthy of censure, but did not consider it fraudulent or dishonest. Michael B. Redmond was subsequently appointed the following May, but he left a year later in May 1876. Three short terms were served by S. Jackson, who became principal for two months in late 1876, followed by W. Marshall, for the last month of 1876 and finally James Sweetman, who was principal for 1878. William Pattison was appointed in January 1879 and remained the principal until 1896. He was replaced by Samuel Flinn. Workmistresses Miss Margaret Pattison and Francis (Fannie) Flinn were appointed in 1894 and 1896 respectively. Two applicants were refused – a Miss Cole for workmistress in 1890, because of the small amount of time devoted to needlework and Jane Hanan as monitress in 1895, as she was over the prescribed age (sixteen years). Revd G.N. Smith was pro-term manager in the absence of Revd Galbraith at the turn of the century. In 1876, the school changed its name from Enniskerry to Powerscourt National School. In the 1901 census, there is no mention of the Pattison family, but Fannie Flinn (age twenty-five) is listed as being in Powerscourt in 1901, and her husband Samuel (age thirty-one) gives the occupation of National School Teacher. By 1911, they had left the village and were residing in Dublin.

Enniskerry No. 2 National School

Soon after Powerscourt's application, Revd Thomas O'Dwyer applied for National School status for a school being housed in the old fever hospital on Kilgarron Hill. Lord Powerscourt was named as patron and Thomas O'Dwyer P.P. named as manager.

The application stated that there was one room in the building in use as a school, which was well lit, 20ft 2ins by 18ft. The application was for Mary Ryan, aged nineteen years, and the school, since opening in February 1869 had an average attendance of 21.6 boys and 20.8 girls. A note on the rear confirms that a salary of £14 would be payable to Mary Ryan from 1 March 1869, and the school was given the roll number 10177. The new school was given books for fifty pupils. The report on the application highlights some points of interest. Three other rooms in the house are occupied by families in Lord Powerscourt's employment. Communication with the Protestant rector did not prompt a reply. Lord Powerscourt, through written communication, undertook to erect wooded structures as offices outside if required, and stated that:

> … he would probably find a site for a new school house if this school succeeds in reference to attendance, etc, for the school will accommodate a considerable number of children who cannot otherwise share the advantages of National Education.

This indeed happened. The minute books stated that in May 1871, there was a temporary change of house pending the erection of a new school house, although it wasn't until 1875 that the new school house, near or on the site of the present library in Enniskerry, was complete and running as a school, with a new roll number of 11353.

The minute books record that on 15 December 1875 there was a note from Lord Powerscourt agreeing to become patron of the new school. The applicant (Revd Thomas O'Dwyer) was requested by the Board to say whether they were to enter Lord Powerscourt on the books as Patron. O'Dwyer replied that he only intended Lord Powerscourt to become joint patron with him. On 21 December, O'Dwyer requested that Lord Powerscourt's name be withdrawn as joint patron.

Jeremiah Golden was named as the principal in the minute books from November 1875, having recently left Curtlestown. A previous principal, Mary Hayden, was dismissed for insufficient answering at exams in March 1873. An application in 1878 was submitted for aid for assistant teacher Annie Golden. The report on this application stated that the school can accommodate 106, and that it had 114 on the rolls, with 80 present on the day of the visit – the low attendance was attributed to 'an epidemic among the pupils'. Mary Dempsey and Eliza Dempsey were named as monitors. Two of the Golden children are named in the minutes. A salary was withdrawn from Michael Golden in 1896 for unsatisfactory answering on results and special courses. In 1898, the manager was informed that Miss Mary Golden did not qualify for the conditions laid down by the English Education department for entrance to training college, as she did not serve as a teacher or monitor in Enniskerry.

The end of Jeremiah Golden's career has a high point and a low point. Having attended a course in Albert Model Farm in Glasnevin, he decided in 1884 to establish a school garden at the school in Enniskerry. Because of the small amount of space Lord Powerscourt gave instructions to have a portion of the wood cut out to extend the space available, resulting in a garden of one rood and twenty perches (0.15 hectares). The school garden was recognised by the Board in April 1886, and by 1897, Jeremiah Golden was testifying to the Commission on Manual and Practical Instruction as an example of good practice in school gardens associated with National Schools.[29] The school garden at Enniskerry was considered one of the best in the country. The pupils tended to the garden each day from 12 to 12.30, during recreation time, each class taking a day in turn, with the girls in a separate section of the garden. When asked about the expense of setting up the greenhouse, he stated that he got the wood from old windows at the Glencree reformatory and glazed them himself, and used wood from Powerscourt demesne and erected the greenhouse himself. His pride in his pupils is evident in the testimony. At one point, he produces a list from a boy named Thomas Watson who was a pupil of his and who now maintains his own cottage garden. The list is the results of the sales of vegetables from his garden for 1896. Elsewhere he mentions he had recently sent a boy to the agent for Powerscourt for employment, based on his experience in the school garden.

It is sad then to relate that Mr Golden's career with the National School did not end well, with his salary being withdrawn in June 1905. The final note in the minute books for the school reads:

> Inspector states that Mr Golden late teacher injured the school garden by mutilating about a dozen rose trees.
> Late teacher Mr Golden entitled to pension of £35 per annum.

The Golden family appear in the 1901 census, with Jeremiah (age fifty-seven) and Annie (aged fifty-four) listed as National School teachers living in Enniskerry village. By 1911, the family had left the village and were living in Kilmainham, Dublin.

Other National Schools

Two other National Schools existed in the area. In Powerscourt parish, Annacrivey was associated with the Board from 1886. The school was housed in a large two-storey house, in good condition and had one schoolroom, 40ft by 16ft. The teacher's name was Phillip O'Connor, aged fifty-four, and his assistant was his daughter, Anne, aged thirty-two. The report on the application queried use of the school for divine Service every Sunday.

The Dargle School (Roll Number 982) in the parish of Delgany, townland of Tinnehinch was taken into connection by the Board in 1833. The teacher's name at the time was Miss Anastasia Duffy, and the correspondent was James Grattan, Bray. The school did not last long. Miss Duffy became ill in 1846, and the school was closed, after a substitute left. The school was struck off the register in 1848, as it was permanently closed from 1 June 1846.

Returns to Annual Reports of Enquiry

Each year, there was a report of the Commissioners of the Board of Education which detailed the numbers attending each school, grants made, etc. These essentially summarise the range of entries in the minute books and issues which arose during the year. The numbers on the roll books for the National Schools in Powerscourt parish, derived from the 3rd report[30] published in 1837 to the 65th report,[31] published in 1899 are shown in Figure 12.

The numbers for Curtlestown show a sharp decline in March 1847, from 130 to 47, although this had mostly recovered by 1849, and a sharp increase in numbers in the early 1860s, attributed previously to the presence of a new teacher. The establishment of a National School in Enniskerry, along with the movement off the rural parts of the parish over this time, as discussed later, meant that Enniskerry became the largest school

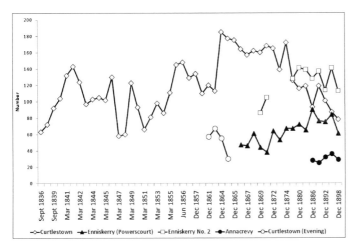

Figure 12: National School Pupil Numbers for schools in Powerscourt parish 1836-1898. (Filled shapes represent schools managed by Established Church clergy; hollow shapes represent schools managed by Roman Catholic Church clergy.)

in the parish from 1874 onwards. The returns for this school during the transition from one building to another were not recorded.

IMPACT OF EDUCATION ON THE POPULACE

A snapshot of the education of the parish is not available until the 1841 census, which reports that number of people over five years old who can read and write, read only and neither read nor write is 1,029, 491 and 1,081 respectively.[32] Levels of illiteracy are higher in rural areas, where more than one in every two people are illiterate (Table 3). In the village, three quarters of the population over five are literate.

By 1861, much more detailed data was collected in the census returns. The 1861 census is considered one of the most impressive ever undertaken in the British Isles. Two themes can be discussed. The first is the levels of literacy by age (Figure 13). While these indicate that the rural portions of the parish had a large number of illiterate people, the proportion of literate to illiterate was generally greater than unity. For example, the returns for the rural population over thirty but less than forty (those that would have been between three and thirteen years old when Curtlestown became a National School) stated that 103 could read and write, 19 could read only and 69 could neither read nor write.[33,34] The numbers for the same age group in the village were 23, 2 and 12 respectively. Therefore it would appear that education was having an impact on this community. The large male population of ten to twenty-year-olds in the rural population of Powerscourt in 1861 is partly due to the population of Glencree reformatory (about 240 at this time).

Table 3: Literacy levels as reported in the 1841 Census[35]

In 1841, persons five years old and upwards who can						
	Read and Write		Read Only		Neither Read nor Write	
	M	F	M	F	M	F
Rural	475	330	224	222	465	497
Enniskerry	110	114	16	29	57	62

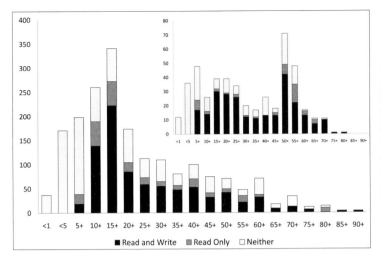

Figure 13: The population distribution in 1861, showing the number in each age bracket who can read and write, read only, neither read nor write in Powerscourt parish rural areas and Enniskerry village (inset). (Information derived from the census of Ireland 1861.)

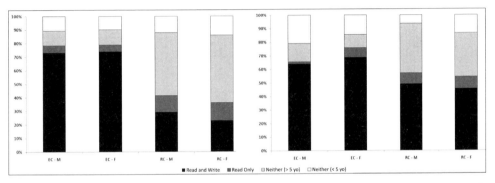

Figure 14: Graph showing the proportion of the population in 1861 in each age bracket who can read and write, read only, neither read nor write (sub-divided by age) in Powerscourt parish rural areas (left) and Enniskerry village (right). EC = Established Church (223 males and 224 females in rural areas; 67 males, 83 females in Enniskerry village); RC = Roman Catholic Church (662 males and 547 females in rural areas; 110 males, 112 females in Enniskerry village). (Information derived from the census of Ireland 1861.)

Secondly, the levels of literacy according to religious denomination were collected in the 1861 census (Figure 14).[36] The figure above shows the proportions of literacy for members of the each of the two main denominations, according to gender and literacy.

The proportions of education by religious denomination show that while education is having an effect on the literacy of the parish, the members of the Protestant community have a much higher level of literacy, markedly so in the rural areas of the parish. (The numbers for the Glencree reformatory are not included in this analysis.)

RELIGION

The discussion of education in the village is largely influenced by the context of religion. In this section, the religious communities in the village are described, in terms of population and places of worship.

Demographics of Faith

One of the significant driving forces behind the establishment of the Board of Education in 1831 was that Catholic emancipation was brought about in the Catholic Relief Act in 1829, precipitated in no small part by the election of Daniel O'Connell in 1828 in Co. Clare. This meant that Roman Catholics could now take a seat in Parliament. There was a need for a literate electorate.[37] Religious information was not gathered in a census until 1861, with both the 1841 and 1851 Census Commissioners being precluded from gathering any information on religion by the Acts that established them. A snapshot from the earlier part of the century is available from the 1835 Commission of Public Instruction in Ireland, which report the data for 'Stagonil, otherwise Powerscourt'.[38] These, along with the returns in the census data from 1861,[39] are shown in Table 4.

The decline in population of Roman Catholics over the period 1834 to 1901 was 1717, whereas that for all Protestant denominations was 1,258. Excluding the population of Glencree Reformatory (approximately 250) which was not present in 1834, this represents a decline of 70 per cent of the population of Roman Catholics over this period and a 76 per cent reduction in the number of Protestant people. The decline in population of the parish as a whole over this period, excluding the numbers in the Glencree Reformatory was about 72 per cent. These values are dependent on the accuracy of the numbers reported for 1834. The 1831 census reported the population of the parish to be 4,538, and the 1841 census, the first to use household forms in place of enumerators requesting information orally from householders, returns the population of the parish as 3,070. Therefore, while the number reported in the 1834 Inquiry are within the range expected, it is probably sufficient to say that the data shows similar percentage reductions in the numbers of Protestant and Roman Catholic communities, with perhaps more reductions for the former. A comparison of the numbers before (1834) and after (1861) the Famine and subsequent emigration that ensued show a reduction in the Protestant community of 63 per cent and 68 per cent for the Roman Catholic community (removing the number reported at Glencree Reformatory, counted as 239 on Oct 18 1861). Again, because of uncertainties in the 1834 numbers, it is concluded that the Famine and emigration affected both communities equally, with a suggestion that it had a slightly greater effect on the Roman Catholic community.

Table 4: Population of parish of Powerscourt, from 1834, 1861 and each subsequent decade to 1901[40, 41, 42, 43, 44, 45]

Year	Established Church/ Protestant Episcopalian	Roman Catholic	Presbyterian	Other Protestant Dissenter	Total
1834	1,656	2,846	4	4	4987[47]
1861	290 male 307 female 597 total	1,012 male 661 female 1,673 total	6 male 9 female 15 total	9 male (Methodist)	1,317 male 977 female 2,294 total
1871	245 male 254 female 499 total	1,070 male 674 female 1,744 total	7 male 6 female 13 total	18 male 24 female 42 total	1,340 male 958 female
1881	235 male 251 female 486 total	929 male 588 female 1,517 total	14 male 11 female 25 total	3 male 3 female 6 total	1,181 male 853 female 2,034 total
1891	202 male 237 female 439 total	860 male 472 female 1,332 total	20 male 15 female 25 total	2 male 3 female 5 total	1,084 male 727 female 1,811 total
1901	167 male 220 female 387 total	679 male 438 female 1,117 total	4 male 6 female 10 total	3 male 6 female 9 total	853 male 670 female 1,523 total

Places of Worship

The parish of Powerscourt was formerly called Stagonil, with a church near the castle at Powerscourt, now the site of the house. Mervyn, 7th Viscount, reports that the workman's bell in the yard of the estate came from this church, and bears the inscription:[48]

Edward Wingfield Esq

John Burton, Isaac Harrison

Church wardens 1723

He suggests that the church may have been modified or rebuilt as this bell predates an inscription engraved on the keystone which read:

John Stanley, Anthony Hicks
Churchwardens 1736

Given the date, modification/rebuilding is plausible, as it coincides with the building of the modern house. The church is marked on Roque's map (1760) of Powerscourt, on both Neville's maps of 1760 and *c.* 1798 and on the 1840 Ordnance Survey map (Chapter 1). By the time the 25 inch map was published towards the end of the century, it is marked as a ruin. The burgeoning population of the early part of the nineteenth century meant that the location of the church was causing problems, as recounted by Mervyn, 7th Viscount in 1904:[49]

A few years before 1857, when I came of age, in consequence of the demesne being on Sundays filled with people attending divine Service, who used to tie up their horses to the trees in the avenue, and whose carriages filled the old stable yard, destroying all privacy, my mother and her husband Frederick, fourth Marquis of Londonderry, determined as my guardians to build a new Parish Church outside the demesne, nearer to the Enniskerry and more conveniently situated for parishioners and also to make the demesne more private.

The new church was located opposite the main gate at Powerscourt, and the foundation stone was laid by the 7th Viscount, on the day of his majority, 13 October 1857. The ceremony was covered by the *Illustrated London News*, which reported:[50]

Next was deposited in a cavity within the foundation-stone, the current gold and silver coins of the realm, together with a copy of one of the Dublin journals, and an inscription on parchment hermetically sealed up in a glass bottle. The following is the inscription:- This foundation stone of the new church to be dedicated to the service of God and in honour of St. Patrick, hereafter to be the parish church of Powerscourt, to be built at the sole expense of Elizabeth, Marchioness of Londonderry, is laid by Mervyn, Viscount Powerscourt, in the presence of the Lord Archbishop of Dublin and the clergy and inhabitants of Enniskerry, this 13th day of October, in the year of Grace, 1857. Joshua Barnard, Rector; Charles McDonogh, Curate; John Buckley and Wm Bunn, Churchwardens; John Nortion [*sic*], of London, Architect.

The young Viscount touched the mortar with a silver trowel, which together with a silver mallet, were presented to him by his tenants for the occasion. The silver came from the Wicklow mines, and the handle was made from a yew tree said to have been planted

Figure 15: Drawing of church of Powerscourt which accompanied a report on the laying of the foundation stone on 21 November 1857. The church that was actually built was much smaller, and had a copper roof.

by St Kevin at Glendalough.[51] The *Illustrated London News* article is accompanied by a sketch of the planned church (Figure 15). It is very much larger in size than the one that was completed in 1859, and shows the spire constructed in stone or slated (as it ultimately was), rather than copper. An *Irish Times* article in October 1859 stated that:

> The gallant Viscount Powerscourt has … determined to present a purse, with one hundred guineas to the couple who shall be fortunate enough to be first joined together in the bonds of wedlock in the handsome new church of Enniskerry, which is now being erected.

The copper spire would ultimately lead to the delay of the consecration of the church until 1863, as the Ecclesiastical Commissioners were not satisfied with the use of slate. The spire was covered in copper after much discussion between the parish and the commissioners, and the church was finally consecrated three years after completion.

To restrict burials at Powerscourt in future, the Viscount 'requested Mr William Buckley, the then innkeeper of the Powerscourt Arms Hotel Enniskerry, who was then churchwarden, to furnish me with a list of the parishioners … the burials in the old churchyard[52] are restricted to those families who had rights prior to 1869.' The slates and windows were removed and the church left as a ruin.

The Roman Catholic community were until 1859 part of the parish of Bray, with a local curate housed in Curtlestown, near the school. Mervyn, 7th Viscount, reported similar problems with the Roman Catholic community using the burial ground in Powerscourt grounds, at the ancient site of Churchtown:

> The Roman Catholics had formerly a burial-ground inside the demesne also, at Churchtown, where are the ruins of an ancient chapel. This old burial ground was very full, and at every funeral, the bones of those who had been buried there before were turned up in digging new graves. There were also terrible scenes sometimes at funerals passing to it and coming past Powerscourt House, etc. Very often those bearing coffins were drunk, and I myself have seen a coffin dropped upon the road near the farmyard, and bursting open, the remains being exposed to view.

Churchtown was marked (without annotation of graveyard or church ruin) on the Nevilles' maps, and the graveyard and church (in ruins) is marked on the 1840 Ordnance survey map, almost due west of Charleville House, in Powerscourt Demesne. He arranged with the Revd Thomas O'Dwyer to provide a 2-acre site near the church at Curtlestown if the quarter acre graveyard at Churchtown could be closed. O'Dwyer had to bring the proposal to the church's Privy Council, and according to Mervyn, 7th Viscount:[53]

> … stated on oath that the burial ground was within a hundred yards of Powerscourt House, and that the smell from it was perfectly pestilential! On this evidence an order was given that it should be closed.

When Powerscourt queried the priest about his testimony, given the graveyard is a mile from the house, he said that the priest replied, 'Oh! I thought you would like it'. The arrangement clearly suited both parties.

The Roman Catholic community in the village had previous worshipped in a barn belonging to Mrs Dixon, who also had a small inn for travellers near the village. During the minority of the 7th Viscount, his great-uncle, Revd William Wingfield and his maternal grandfather, 3rd Earl of Roden administered the estate. Both his mother and the Earl were evangelical Protestants, and are said to have been opposed to the granting of the site of a Catholic church. However, when the new Viscount came of age, he granted some land near Knocksink for a site for a new church and parish house, at a rent of a shilling a year. The design by Patrick Byrne was quickly implemented, and the foundation stone was blessed in April 1858, the church dedicated in October 1859 and inaugurated, without its spire in June 1860, three years before the church at Powerscourt gates was to be consecrated.[54]

Clergymen

By the time the new churches were built, clergymen of the earlier part of the century had been replaced. Enniskerry, with its new church, became a Roman Catholic parish in its own right, with the Revd Thomas O'Dwyer as parish priest. Like many clergymen both parishes held over the century, he appears to have been a formidable character. As discussed, he was manager of the National Schools in both Curtlestown and Enniskerry, and as late as 1867 was objecting to the connection of Powerscourt School with the Board of Education, because it had a Protestant master. He appears to have been connected with the parish long before he became parish priest – perhaps as curate. He is named as the correspondent for Curtlestown National School in a note in 12 March 1839.[55] An anecdote about him is recounted by Mervyn, 7th Viscount, who tells the story of when a mob allying themselves to the Fenian uprising in March 1867 marched to Enniskerry:[56]

> This was on the occasion of the culmination of the plots against the Government of the Fenian or Irish Republican Brotherhood. Certain desperate characters had come over to Ireland, adventurers who had taken part in the Civil war between North and South in the United States in 1862 and following years. Fenianism and rebellion had been brewing in Ireland for some time, and in 1864 the Lord Lieutenant, Lord Wodehouse had suppressed and seized the Fenian Newspaper 'The Irish People' and arrested various persons charged with being members of the Fenian Brotherhood, the leader of whom was James Stephens ... in the night before the 25th of March a rising took place in Dublin, and on that morning we heard that a large number of Fenians were marching on Enniskerry. My agent, Mr Posnett, rode up and reported that an armed force some with muskets, some with pikes and other improvised weapons, had appeared there, and that they were met on the road at the bridge near the chapel by the parish priest the Rev Thomas O'Dwyer, who confronted them with a crucifix and commanded them to go back. They obeyed, and turned off to the road near the Scalp, leading to Glencullen, the only damage they had done being to attack a baker's cart and seize all the bread.

A less than happy fate awaited a priest who tried to quell an attack on Powerscourt House during the rebellion of 1798:[57]

> At the time of the rebellion in 1798 an attack was made upon Powerscourt House one very dark night, which was not unexpected by the inhabitants who had had information of the intention of the rebels and were therefore prepared to defend themselves, which they did by firing from the windows. This could only be done at random, as the only light was from a few torches carried by the enemy for the purpose of setting fire to the house. In the meantime the Roman Catholic Priest of the parish had heard what was going on, and hastened to the scene to try and pacify the mob and

induce them to retire. Unfortunately the presence of the clergyman was unknown to those inside the house and one of the shots from the windows unintentionally killed him. This quelled the ferocity of the rebels, who felt that they were the cause of his death, and they retired, but it is a tradition that he, with his dying breath, cursed the Powerscourt family, saying that no lord Powerscourt should live to see his son come of age! There is a saying that the grass would not grow on the spot where he fell, and in that consequence the roadway in front of the house had been widened so that there should be no grass on the fatal spot!

However, despite differences resulting from penal laws and the run-up to Catholic emancipation, which manifested themselves mainly in education, the communities appeared to be a relatively content tenantry. Mervyn, 7th Viscount, stated that no one had ever been evicted on the estate either by him or his father, summarizes this general feeling by using the two previous anecdotes:[58]

> … I write this account because in both the much more serious outbreak in 1798 and in this latter attempt at insurrection in 1867, it is interesting that the feeling among the people at Powerscourt was shewn by the Roman Catholic Priest being the principal agent on the side of law and order, and that the relations between our tenantry and ourselves had always been of a friendly character, which in many parts of Ireland has not been the case.

Another formidable clergyman in the village was the rector of Powerscourt parish, Revd Robert Daly. Daly was an evangelical Protestant, and had a wide variety of interests, including educational and social reform. He was rector from 1814 until 1843, when he was appointed Bishop of Cashel. Daly was a close personal friend of Elizabeth, the widow of the 6th Viscount. Like O'Dwyer, he had an enormous impact on the education of his flock, both in supporting schools directly, through involvement in the Kildare Place Society, and of course in a range of Sunday school and scriptural classes he organised. He came from a wealthy family background, and was evidently well thought of in his community. In an anonymously authored text, written in 1872, an 'old parishioner' recounts many stories of the Revd Daly. Among these were one which describes the friendship between Daly and Lady Powerscourt:[59]

> Lady Rathdowne and Lady Powerscourt, who were residents, were both remarkable for their piety. The latter was very fond of the study of prophecy; she had evening meetings every second Tuesday for the purpose at Powerscourt House, at which Mr Daly presided; when, after tea, she would 'prove him with hard questions'… they were held for three of four consecutive summers by Lady Powerscourt, when she had

her house filled with the most eminent divines of every denomination, in England, Scotland and Ireland.

Later, the parishioner states that Lady Powerscourt 'deserted her ministry and joined 'the meeting of the discontented in Aungier-street'. Another passage refers to the relationship between Revd Daly and his curate:[60]

Mr McK_____ was a great contrast to his rector, being remarkable for the child-like simplicity of his character. Mr Daly used to call him his little wife, and was very fond of him, but was sometimes provoked with him for being so easily imposed upon. He one day lent him an umbrella, as it was raining when he set out to walk to Enniskerry from the Glebe. When he got half way, it stopped raining, and Mr McK_____, meeting a beggar-woman, he gave her sixpence and the umbrella, which he desired her to leave at the Glebe, but which she did not do.

Another line makes reference to the fact that services were held in Powerscourt church by the house except in the winter, when service would be held in Mr Daly had service in the Glebe school house and the curate in the one in Enniskerry:[61]

The old Lord Powerscourt (grandfather to the present Viscount) had offered to light up Powerscourt Avenue with lamps hung from trees, if he would continue the evening service during the winter.

Finally, referring to other denominations:[62]

It may well be imagined that in a parish so well looked after, there was no such thing as dissent. There was not at that time even a Roman Catholic chapel in Enniskerry, and they held their service in a coach-house belonging to one of the lodging houses in the village. A Methodist preacher once held a meeting near the glebe, but when he found out that he had the rector of the parish as one of his audience, he did not come again. Mr Daly said to him, 'I heard you had come to feed my people, and I came to see what sort of food you were giving them.'

Table 5 shows the clergymen present in the parishes over the course of the century, with approximate dates.

Table 5: Clergymen for both Communities over the Nineteenth Century

Established Church/Protestant	Roman Catholic
1814-1843 Robert Daly	Prior to 1817 'A priest not very clerical in his character', according to Rev Robert Daly
	From c. 1816-1817 – Revd Daly C.C. (James Doyle was the parish priest of Bray)
	1834 Patrick Black C.C. Named as the curate on the application for Curtlestown National School. Revd Roche is named as the parish priest.
1846–1867 Joshua Bernard and C. McDonagh, curate. Both named as correspondents for Annacrivey National School, 1866	18 September 1838 John Harman CC Named as correspondent in Curtlestown NS minute books
	12 March 1839 Thomas O'Dwyer. Named as correspondent in Curtlestown NS minute books
1867–1873 Charles McDonagh	1859–1887 Thomas O'Dwyer. Became parish priest on inauguration of new parish at Enniskerry
1874–1905 Henry Galbraith. Notes for Powerscourt National NS state that Revd G.N. Smith (1899) manager in the absence of Galbraith; Rev DE Newcombe recognised as manager from April 1902.	1887–1890 Michael Patterson Minute books for Curtlestown NS and Enniskerry No. 2 NS state that Patterson has 'resigned and left Ireland permanently'
	1890–1907 Charles Cuddihy

THE REFORMATORY AT GLENCREE

At the edge of the parish, the former military barracks at Glencree in the townland of Aurora was certified as a reformatory school in April 1859.[63] The school and 100 acres of land was granted by lease from Lord Powerscourt. The school opened with about 175 pupils, quickly rising to 228 by the end of the year,[64] and peaking to a maximum of over 300 by the early 1870s.[65] An annual report each year from the inspectorate of reformatory reported on the number of boys, admissions, costs, health, etc. In the decade after opening, the inspector was fulsome in praise of the school manager, Revd Mr Lynch, and his staff in their running of the school, stating that the conditions of the building and nature of the landscape meant that the 'difficulties … which the Revd Mr Lynch has had to encounter, and has surmounted, are all but incredible'.[66]

Early reports demonstrate that the building was not fit for purpose; described as 'unsound', with just one room habitable when it opened.[67] However, after initial immediate renovation, the site had a series of new additions, including a new dormitory (1861), with an infirmary and schoolrooms (1862), a smithy (1865), a gas-house (1866), a bakehouse (1871), and a stone church replacing the former wooden structure (1873). The staff lived in the central house, formerly the barrack, with the married staff and tradesmen living in houses built in land around the reformatory. Requests for a play hall from the late 1870s could not be completed due to lack of funds. The living conditions were not good, with poor bed furniture and mattresses in the large dormitories, although these were finally replaced by 1880. The entire reformatory was lit by gas made on site, but was poorly heated, with only the new church being heated by hot water pipes in 1880, although there were plans at that stage to heat the schoolrooms and dormitory by the same manner.

The discipline of the reformatory was, according to several reports, not severe. A wide range of trades were taught in order to provide a means of employment for the boys after they left the reformatory. Of the 239 boys present in 1861, twenty-four were being trained in tailoring, twenty-five in shoemaking, seventeen in cabinet making and carpentry. The rest were involved in agriculture, which at that stage meant reclaiming the bog land around the reformatory. Within fifteen years, the number of trades had expanded significantly, to include stonecutting, quarrying, gas-making, upholstery, glazing, cart-making, blacksmith works, harness making, boot-making, all supported by a wide range of instruments. These were powered by waterworks, supplied by a reservoir above the reformatory, still present today. Several master tradesmen were on the staff. While the industrial work made money for the school, its funds were continually drained by the cost of transporting the materials to and from the location. A report in 1870 stated that the cost of haulage alone for a ton of coal cost 10s. The reformatory also had an extensive farm, with pigs, sheep, horses and cattle. Education, provided by two teachers, with a third trained by the Board of Education arriving in 1875, consisted of reading, writing and arithmetic, with some of the boys learning more advanced topics if it was necessary for their trades. While many reports acknowledge that it was difficult to teach reading and writing to the older boys, a policy of requiring a certain level of literacy before a boy could be released on licence, introduced in 1874, meant that the boys were 'more attentive than formerly'.[68]

The health of the boys was generally reported as satisfactory, given the large number of inmates. A small pox outbreak in 1871, caused either by a visitor to the school or a visit by one of the boys to his home at Christmas, ultimately resulted in five deaths. In 1874, the health of the school was reported as very satisfactory, but there were four deaths by accident, when an earthen bank collapsed on a group of boys working underneath.

The boys attending the reformatory generally did so for a period of several years – usually five – although they could be released on licence when they had served half their time. This was considered by the managers the time required for the boys to be 'reformed'. Many of the inmates had lost one or both parents. An inquiry, separate to the annual reports, in 1870 listed the boys detained, and their circumstances.[69] The offences were typically larceny, with others listed misdemeanour, pick-pocketing, attempt at felony, and some as minor as 'stealing from parents', 'stealing fruit', and 'stealing eggs'. The last case was boy who received a sentence from Limerick Petty Sessions Court on 2 May 1864 of one month in gaol and five years at the reformatory. He was aged just thirteen on conviction. In 1870, 129 boys were admitted, eight under ten years old, thirty-nine between ten and twelve, forty-six between twelve and fourteen, and thirty-six between fourteen and sixteen. Of these, 103 were first offences.

On release, they were often monitored. One of the early monitors was Monsieur Ferdinand Vernet, assistant to the manager at the time, who visited the boys who got positions after leaving, and is credited by an early report of influencing the Town Council of Dublin to increase the grant received per boy from 2s to 3s 6d. Many of the boys revisited after departure (considered by one inspector to be a measure of a good school), and the school was available to them if they became homeless. The monitoring system did not appear to be as close in later years, due to pressures on the system, and this is given to be the cause for a number of the boys reoffending. There were several cases of 'success', however, with reports of the vast majority of boys 'doing well' after release. For the years 1867–1869, 243 boys were discharged. Sixty-four went to employment or service, and fifty-nine returned to friends. One hundred emigrated, three were sent to sea and thirteen enlisted. Four were specially discharged, probably due to infectious illness. Of these, three were since dead, 205 were doing well, seven doubtful, nine were subsequently convicted of crime and nineteen were unknown.

Over the subsequent three years 1870–1872, 217 boys were discharged with 194 doing well and nine reconvicted. The number was much higher in the next three years; of the 310 boys released, forty-one were reconvicted. The pressures of the increasing numbers in the system were beginning to take their toll. Glencree was the largest reformatory in the system until the 1890s, by which time its numbers had reduced again to about 200.[70]

The reformatory was managed by a priest, with an assistant clergyman, and about seventeen lay brothers. There were several tradesmen, some farmhands and teachers also employed. The names of the managers are given in Table 6.

Table 6: Managers of Glencree Reformatory 1859–1900

Time Range	Manager
1859–1865	Revd F.J. Lynch
1866–1871	Revd Laurence P. Fox
1871–1876	Revd Matthew Shinnors
1876–1880	Revd M. Gaughren
1880–1884	Revd D. McIntyre
1884–c. 1893	Revd J. King
1894–c. 1900	Revd Charles Cox

In the 1901 census, the returns show that the manager was Thomas Furlong, aged forty-nine, who was assisted by Joseph Maher and thirteen lay teachers. There were 171 boys resident, the youngest, John Russell, just ten years old. There were eight boys between eleven and twelve, fifty-four between thirteen and fourteen, fifty-three between fifteen and sixteen and fifty-five between seventeen and eighteen. Seventeen of the boys cannot read or write, and eleven can read only. The census shows several houses associated with the reformatory, housing Stephen Barry and family, blacksmith; Denis Moran and his sister, tailor; Joseph Dunne and family, with six children including a son John (age twenty), who was a stone mason; a second Dunne listing including another John Dunne (age seventeen), stone mason; Isaac Smyth, agricultural labourer, his wife Mary who was a dairy maid, and their sons Edward and William, who were stonemasons and William O'Byrne, who lists his occupation as musician (bandmaster). One final residence houses a Mrs Foley, who does not list an occupation.

SUMMARY

Education and religion were the dominant forces in the daily lives of people during the nineteenth century, and the two were inextricably linked. However, the establishment of the Board of Education, and the subsequent connection to the Board of Curtlestown, Powerscourt and Enniskerry National Schools resulted in huge positive impact on the education of the youth of the village, evidenced by improving rates of literacy over the course of the century. The final chapter considers other impacts of the people, through the presence of Lord Powerscourt – namely the development of agriculture, society in the village and the toll of the Great Famine.

3

LIFE IN THE PARISH OF POWERSCOURT

Census of Ireland 1821–1901 – Agriculture: Snapshots in Time –
The Famine Years – Health – Post-Famine Life – Summary

The nineteenth century was one of great change in Ireland. After a peak in the early part of the century, the population declined due to emigration, and with the coming of the Famine, death. The number of people living off the land reduced substantially. These national trends are reflected in the lives of the people of the parish of Powerscourt. Details of farming practices, the quality of life of people living in the area, and the impact of the Famine on the local population can be derived from Census data and local accounts from archives. The century was a difficult one, but population decline did lead to an improvement in the life of the people towards the end of the century.

CENSUS OF IRELAND 1821–1901

A national census of Ireland was taken every decade from 1821. While the individual returns of all census prior to 1921 were pulped or destroyed in a fire during the Civil War, summaries of population returns and other data collected, often to townland level, are available through House of Commons Parliamentary Papers. Information up to and including 1891 was arranged by parish, with population of townlands within a parish recorded from 1841 onwards. In 1901, the arrangement was slightly different, but the townland data was aggregated to compare parish information to the nineteenth century census data. Enniskerry was identified as a village in the 1821 census and

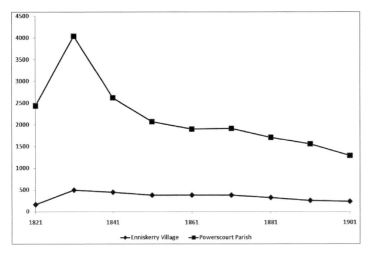

Figure 16: Population profile for Powerscourt parish (rural) and Enniskerry Village for each decade from 1821 to 1901 derived from census data.

Figure 17: Proportion of population of Powerscourt (rural and village) who were male and female, derived from census data.

from 1831 was listed separately to the other townlands in Powerscourt, which were summarised as 'Powerscourt rural'.

Demographic Information

The population of the parish of Powerscourt and Enniskerry village determined in each census is shown in Figure 16.[1, 2, 3, 4, 5, 6, 7, 8, 9] Some degree of scepticism might be held about the 1821 and 1831 data, which were obtained by interview and it has been argued that they under-represent the population by as much as 5 per cent. From 1841, the data was obtained by enumerator forms, similar to the situation in modern times.

While both the population of the rural parts of the parish and the village declined from a peak in 1831, the rate of decline in the rural areas was much faster, reflecting that of the county as a whole. For each decade from 1821, the proportion of the total number of people (rural and village) living in the village increased from 6 per cent to a peak of 17 per cent in 1871, levelling off to 15 per cent in 1901. Therefore there was a considerable shift off the land during this period. The ratio of male to females in the parish was 1:1 in 1831 (2,262 male: 2,276 female) and this ratio steadily increased in line with the overall population decrease, to a maximum of three men for every two women in 1891 (Figure 17); although the male population from 1861 onwards is boosted by the numbers present in Glencree Reformatory (typically 200–300). However, within this overall population change, the ratio of male to females in the village remained around the 1:1 level, with a slight relative increase in the number of women by 1891 apparent (1:1.2).

This data indicates that the population decline in rural areas of the parish was sharper for females, and may indicate a movement of women and families off the land to more urban environments. This was observed throughout the county – the proximity to Dublin meant that Wicklow's female population dropped more sharply, as women took domestic jobs in the city.[10]

A convenient method of tracking the population change is by examining the townland populations over the period 1831 to 1901. The townlands of the parish are shown in the map in Figure 18. They are grouped as follows:

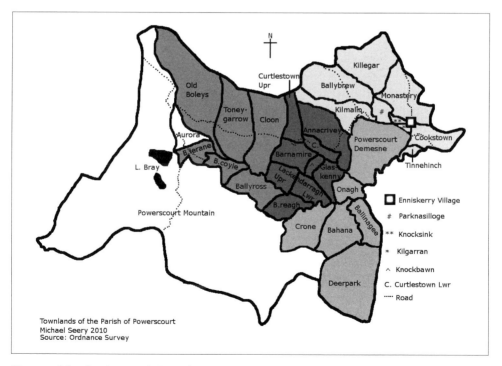

Figure 18: Map showing population reduction 1841-1901 in groups of townlands, from the darkest shade (77 per cent reduction), through to the lightest shade (69 per cent, 55 per cent, 40 per cent reduction respectively), derived from census data.

(i) The lands of Glencree, excluding the townland of Aurora which contained the Reformatory since 1859 and the townland of Powerscourt Mountain, which did not have any significant population over the period.

(ii) The lands around Curtlestown, including townlands Curtlestown Upper and Lower, Annacrivey, Barnamire, Glaskenny, and others.

(iii) The lands including and to the south of Powerscourt Demesne, including Onagh, Ballinagee, Bahana and Crone.

(iv) The lands around Enniskerry Village, including Kilmalin, Ballybrew, Killegar, Monastery and Cookstown, as well as small townlands in the village.

This analysis indicates that the largest population decrease, of about 77 per cent, was observed in the aggregated population of townlands around Curtlestown, probably due to the agglomeration of a lot of small farms into three or four larger farms over the period.[11] This is followed by a decrease of about 69 per cent in the townlands around Glencree and lower decreases in the townlands around the demesne (55 per cent) and finally townlands around Enniskerry village (40 per cent). This would emphasise the point that there was a movement off the land over the course of the century, with the reduction in the 'urban' areas of the parish less dramatic. Populations for individual townlands are given in the Appendix.

Housing Stock and Quality
Similar deductions can be drawn from the number of houses over the period 1841 to 1901. Grouping together the townlands as described above, the same trend in the drop in the number of houses is observed. In the region around Curtlestown, with the

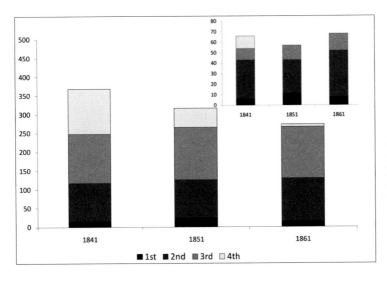

Figure 19: Classification of housing stock in the rural townlands of Powerscourt parish and Enniskerry village (inset) over the years 1841–1861, derived from census data.

largest population decrease, the number of houses fell from ninety-one to thirty-six, a fall of about 60 per cent over the sixty years. In the region around Glencree, the number of houses fell from ninety-five to fifty-three, a fall of about 45 per cent. The region of the parish around the demesne and south of the demesne saw its number of houses fall from fifty-two to thirty-seven, a fall of about 30 per cent, and finally the number of houses in and around the village fell from 206 to 158, a fall of under 25 per cent. The decline in population in the rural parts of the parish is matched by the largest proportionate decline in the number of houses in these areas. However, the relative standard of housing quality of the parish improved over this time. While data is not available at townland level, from the 1841 census, each house in the parish was ranked according to its quality, and numbers reported. The class ranking is described in Table 7.

Table 7: Classification of Houses in Census 1841–1861

Class	Description
1st	Superior house to other classes
2nd	House with five to nine rooms, with windows, such as 'a good farmhouse or in towns in a small street'
3rd	House built of mud, two to four rooms, with windows
4th	House built of mud, one room, no windows. In 1871, this class was subdivided into one-room brick or stone house (4A) and a one room mud house (4B), but reverted back to the original classification in 1881.

The proportion of houses in each class for the rural parts of the parish and Enniskerry village are shown in Figure 19. It is evident that the decline in numbers of houses in the rural area over the period 1841–1901 was mainly a result of decline in the number of 4th class houses, which had all but disappeared by 1861. The village saw the elimination of 4th class houses by 1851 with a concurrent rise in the number of second class houses. Data from 1871 onwards was not reported at parish level.

Occupation

Census returns also gave information on the occupations of the people. As is to be expected, the predominant occupation of people was agriculture. In 1831, 1,082 males were twenty years of age or older in the parish (including the village).[12] Of these, 611 (57 per cent) were listed in the census as being labourers employed in agriculture and 103 (10 per cent) being sole farmers. Just fifty were occupiers employing labourers (5 per cent). The remainder of the men were employed in retail trade/handicraft/ Masters/workmen (11 per cent) or were capitalists, bankers, professional and other educated men (5 per cent). About 8 per cent of the male population over twenty were servants. The 1831 census only provides information on the number of female servants – no other occupation is listed. 290 women were listed as servants, about 10 per cent of the entire female population in the parish.

The 1841 and 1851 census data recorded occupational information slightly differently. Occupations were assigned to one of nine categories – for example 'Ministering to Physical Wants (Food)', which included farmers, servants and labourers, gardeners etc. Responses included anybody over fifteen years old and were in these cases given by gender. Table 8 summarises the response for 1841 and 1851.

Table 8: Classification of occupations according to Census data for 1841 and 1851 for Powerscourt parish (rural and village)[13, 14]

Persons (fifteen years and upwards) classified as ministering to		1841	1851
1. Physical Wants			
Food	M	617	484
	F	28	31
Clothing	M	40	24
	F	41	37

Lodgings, furniture, machinery &c.	M	69	77
	F	1	2
Health	M	5	3
	F	3	2
Charity	M	0	0
	F	0	0
2. Moral Wants			
Justice	M	12	20
	F	0	0
Education	M	4	3
	F	4	3
Religion	M	3	2
	F	0	0
Unclassified	M	50	79
	F	159	142

By 1861, the system had changed again, with only occupation by family being recorded. 182 families were classified as being chiefly employed in agriculture; fifty-four as being engaged in manufacture, trade, etc and 134 assigned to other occupations.[15] Census from 1871 onwards did not record occupation at parish level.

While the changing nature of data collection frustrates a comparison of occupations across the decades, it can be concluded that the reduction in population and the improvement in housing stock correlates with the reduction in agriculture as an occupation. The movement off the land was affecting this occupation most significantly.

611 men over twenty were recorded as being employed by agriculture in 1831 and a similar number over fifteen years old were employed in 1841, falling to 484. The decline represents a fall of 20 per cent between 1831 and 1851, even before accounting for the additional five year age bracket included in the later figures.

AGRICULTURE: SNAPSHOTS IN TIME

The role of people living off the land can be placed in some local context by considering sources written at key stages during the century. The first was by Robert Fraser, who provided many agricultural details in his Statistical Account of Co. Wicklow, published at the start of the century in 1801. The second is data recording the years in the run up to the Famine, in the form of returns provided to the Poor Inquiry Commissioners in 1836, which detailed the conditions of agriculture workers and farming at the time. Finally, the Famine Relief Commission papers in the years of the Famine itself give some information on how the locality was responding to the disastrous implications of crop failure.

Agriculture at the Turn of the Century

Robert Fraser visited the county in 1800, and wrote up his Statistical Account detailing agricultural and industrial practices as well as outlining some conditions of labourers.[16] He devoted a section to Powerscourt, having spoken to a local man whose judgement he valued. Fraser considered the area unusual, its 'grandeur and beauty' aside, because of the high number of yeoman tenants living in the parish. However, he does not hide disappointment at the lack of innovation in agricultural practices being carried out in the locality, blaming it on the long leases (thirty-one years or three lives) afforded by Powerscourt:[17]

> Easy rents may have produced a careless indolence and hence an aversion to enterprise. The landlord having but little interest in such estates, and less power over such tenants, is himself checked from any spirit of improvement, upon such contingent property …

He concedes the tenants are lucky with the soil, and 'fine pasturage it affords, enables them to maintain their families with ease, and they make little or no use of the rich marl and limestone gravel, which is almost in every field to be found …'.

While agriculture is the predominant industry in the locality, Fraser notes that most farmers would manufacture frise (a rough woollen cloth) and sell the excess they did not use. Some families in the locality made 'the coarsest kind of felt hats' which were sold for 3s or 4s each. There was no scale in the manufacture to render it beneficial. Fraser comments that:[18]

A few women in the parish, when supplied with flax by the gentry, spin it into an inferior kind of yarn, and two or perhaps three weavers can be found, who will work it into sheeting, rubbering and towels, and at a rate (every expense considered) which in the end exceeds the value for which articles of same quality can be procured at a Dublin shop.

Fraser also reports on the conditions of labourers in the parish. From November to May, men could earn 10*d* per day, and 1*s* during the summer months. Children, depending on their age and strength, could earn 5 to 6½*d* per day. Farmers generally fed their labourers, but in these cases paid them less. Food was chiefly potatoes for eight or nine months of the year and for the remainder, oaten meal, and occasionally household wheaten bread. The usual price of potatoes, when purchased, was formerly from 2*s* 6*d* to 3*s* per hundred weight, but in the year Fraser surveyed, the prices had been very high. Flour, ground in America, was used to make 'stirabout', a variation on porridge. Where possible, labourers who did not have their own cow were freely provided skim milk and butter milk.

Most labourers had no land attached to their houses, some had small plots, 'from half an acre to five, seldom so much'. Those that didn't could rent a little, wherever they can get it sufficiently convenient to their place of residence. There were inconsistencies in the rents paid for land, a problem which was to remain up until Griffith's land valuation fifty years later:[19]

> When he has the good fortune to hold his cottage and some land immediately from a gentleman or capital farmer, he seldom pays more for it than it is really worth, but when he holds it from a petty farmer, he pays from double to treble the real value of the land: instances more than one occur in which a farmer, who represents his whole farm of 40 acres to be not worth 25s per acre lets the worst possible half acre without any house for two guineas a year, and saddles him besides with a very unjust proportion of the tithe and county cess.

Agriculture and Life Before the Famine

The growing poverty and lack of employment in Ireland resulted in a Poor Inquiry being established in the 1830s to examine the suitability of establishing a similar system to the English workhouses here. As part of the inquiry, the Poor Law Commissioners examined several witnesses in various localities to evaluate living and working conditions. One of those interviewed was Revd Robert Daly, of Powerscourt parish. The questions covered a range of issues around agriculture, conditions of labour and living conditions. From the evidence, the following snapshot of pre-Famine living conditions of the locality can be drawn.

A typical labourer in the parish of Powerscourt would have a farmer as an immediate landlord, paying rent of about £2 to £4 per annum plus the cost of any land. Most of them also rented land, whose cost varied widely depending on quality, ranging from £6 to 10s per acre. The cabins were generally in poor repair, usually made of mud and stone. A condition of their tenancy was that they would work for their landlord at about 10d to 1s per day, or 6d with food, the same amount given by Fraser over thirty years earlier. Employment was low between Christmas and Spring, and before the May harvest, and altogether a typical labourer could earn about £15 to £20 per year. Wages were paid in cash, with deductions taken for rent and land.

In general, housing was not shared between families, except in some cases close to the village where houses were scarce. There had been some emigration – 'five or six young respectable persons' per year in the years prior to 1835, who had gone to Van Diemen's Land and America. The general condition of the poor has deteriorated in the last twenty years, owing to a surge in population. The typical diet of the labouring class was potatoes and milk, with herrings and milk and a small amount of bacon. Herring in the locality was usually provided from the fisheries at Arklow.[20]

A more personal glimpse – perhaps rose-tinted – of pre-Famine life in the parish can be drawn from the account of Catherine M. O'Connell, who visited in 1844, and was one of the last travel narrators to write about Ireland before the Famine. She describes visiting a cottage on her way from the Dargle to Powerscourt Waterfall:[21]

> We enter one cottage, and its pretty exterior covered with woodbine, roses and ivy, correspond with the neatness within; the only inmate received us with a ready smile, and dusting the straw-bottomed chairs asked us to be seated; she looked a picture of cheerful happiness she acknowledged she felt; her husband had plenty of work, was 'a dacent, quiet boy', her children were at school, and they had a good lease of their 'little place'. She brought a cup of milk for an English lady of our party, and stoutly refused any remuneration telling us with a tact which I gave her great credit for, that she had a sister in London married to an Englishman, and that 'his people were very kind to Mary'…
>
> The path to this cottage was through pretty garden, abundance of common flowers blooming in the borders, and the little gate in an un-Irish style, in good repair. There was no poverty here, the flowers plainly said so.

Relations between tenantry and landlords appear, anecdotally at least, to have been good. As mentioned above, the standard term of lease was long, and the 7th Viscount talked in his memoirs how neither he nor his father had ever evicted a tenant. However, one event that came to national media attention in 1840 when a mob destroyed a fence that had been built along the boundaries of the Deerpark, which had 'the twofold purpose of giving employment to the poor and improving his Lordship's estate'.[22] On returning to rebuild the fence under the direction of the estate manager Mr Robert Sandys, supported by fifty of the Wicklow constabulary, the workmen were again confronted by a 'dense body of men, women and children numbering upwards of 500, armed with spades, shovels and sithes'. The ringleader was Garrett O'Toole, 'a well-known character'. The report continues:[23]

> They then shouted, 'We have been driven from our land and property, and before Good Friday we will be driven into the sea for our religion!' They called on the policemen to begin and 'fire, if they dared; that they had had seen one rebellion, and outlived it.'

The mob levelled the fence to the ground, and the article states that the workmen had informed the mob that the fence building would resume.

A second incident arose the following year over turf rights on the lands between Powerscourt and Charleville – which may have involved the enclosure of common land – with a request from Powerscourt stop to breaching the peace, and that his aim was to improve the land. Perhaps reflecting on the previous year's events, he notes that he is 'inclined to think that tenants have been instigated to this course by malicious persons'.

In general, however, there does seem to have been good relations between Powerscourt and the tenantry. At the retirement in 1845 of Richard Sandys, who was the agent for the estate, a printed document[24] was circulated listing over 150 names of well-wishers and adding that 'here follows upwards of 250 names of tenantry of every denomination'. The names of Enniskerry occupants are listed in the Appendix. Sandys, in his reply to the meeting said that he had 'a warm and grateful regard of those of *every rank and denomination*' (his emphasis) and that in his thirty years as an agent connected to the tenantry, he had found:[25]

> … integrity and punctuality, even in the humblest in the payment of their rent – gratitude with which they appreciated all the kindness and likeability of their lamented landlord –peaceable conduct, good order and kindly feelings that pervaded them all…

THE FAMINE YEARS

The Famine years 1845–1847 devastated the country generally. The toll on North Wicklow, because of its proximity to Dublin, may have been ameliorated because of migration to the city.[26] The archives from the Famine Relief Commission give some indication of how the authorities were managing, or at least monitoring, the situation in the locality. The Commission was established in late 1845 in response to the failure of the potato crop in the autumn of that year, and during 1846 local relief committees were established. A committee was established in the parish of Powerscourt in late 1846, with George Cranfield J.P. as chairman and Benjamin Buckley as secretary.[27] The purpose was to communicate to the Commissioners, detailing subscriptions received from locals and outlining requests for support. As an example, the list of subscriptions dated in March 1847 totalled over £120, including contributions from Guardians of Viscount Powerscourt (£50), Robert Sandys (£5), Revd Thomas O'Dwyer (£2), Dr Gray (10s 3d), Dr Rapole (£2) and Henry Monck Mason (£2). The letter requested matched funding of £120 from the Commissioners, stating:[28]

> … we have an extensive mountain tract included within our district where much poverty and destitution prevails. The number of labourers who have been paid by the Inspectors office is 280 – and we supply upwards of two hundred rations, each consisting of a pint of soup and a pound of cooked rice and Indian meal… to persons completely destitute. Under the circumstances I trust that we can be met with some favourable consideration.

There was no response, and Cranfield resubmitted the request the following month asking for an urgent reply, as their own funds were 'almost exhausted'.[29] There are no records to indicate whether money was ever sent. Labourers employed by the Board of Works could expect to earn about 8–10d per day, which was insufficient to support a family. In many cases in the county, there was food available, but people had insufficient money to buy it.[30]

One of the other methods for monitoring the impact of the Famine locally was the use of constabulary reports who summarised the extent of land planted in potatoes. Returns for the parish of Powerscourt were sent in May 1846 by Const. Whittaker of Barnamire.[32] 140 acres were planted in both 1844 and 1845, and this dropped slightly to 132 acres in 1846, with the remainder planted in turnip and rapeseed where potatoes would normally be. For the land around Enniskerry, Constable John Winter of Enniskerry recorded that 149 acres and 156 acres were planted in potatoes in 1844 and 1845 respectively, dropping to 124 acres in 1846, the remainder of the land which was used for potatoes being planted in turnips and oats.[33] (In many parts of Ireland, more than the normal amount of potatoes were planted in the spring of 1846 in the hope of having a sufficient crop.) At the same time, county Inspectors were compiling the returns to send summary information confidentially to Dublin Castle. In answers for the Bray police district, August 1846, the returns showed that the extent of planting of potatoes this year was not completely but the same as previous years and that upwards of three quarters of the crop had been affected – 'no field [is] safe'. While the early crop had been mainly affected, some food was becoming available, a 'small proportion remaining uninjured'.[34] The situation was the same or worse in other districts in the county.

As discussed earlier, the Guardians of Powerscourt employed a large number of labourers during the Famine years in road and estate improvement works. The house and gardens also had a staff whose pay is recorded in 1844 salary books available in the Powerscourt papers.[35] As well as pay, former staff of Powerscourt received a pension of between £2 and £10, which would have been something of a rarity in that time. Employees and annual salary include a steward (James Croghan, £100), a gardener (Alexander Ross, £73 17s), an inspector at Deerpark (Michael McGinty, £50), a forrester (James Ward, £35) a shepard (Robert Walker, £15), a herd ranger (William Roe, £30) and bailiff (William Booth, £8 11s 6d) at Deerpark, a mountain keeper at Kippure (John Eager, £16), a wood ranger at Kilmolin (Terrence Reilly, £14 9s) and seven gatekeepers[36] with salaries ranging from £5 to £21. Other indoor staff included a housekeeper (Mrs Smith, £50), three housemaids (Mary Meyers, first housemaid, £16 and Anne Kirkpatrick, second housemaid, £12, Mary Connell, £10), a dairy maid (Mary Curran, £12) and a house servant (Edward Kearney, £6). A proportion of the house staff's wages was paid in the form of boarding. Along with teaching salaries mentioned earlier, the total expense on salaries for twenty-eight employees was just over £200 for a quarter. Seven of the fourteen signatures of the salaries page could not write. Ten people are listed as receiving pensions, and of the eight signatures, seven are marked with an X.

HEALTH

The toll of poverty before and during the Famine can be measured by the population fall in the parish, which had been declining steadily since 1831, and continued to fall between 1841 and 1851, as described above. In the years before the Famine, the problem for the poor was the gap between availability of stocks from the previous year and the harvest of the current year, and of course during the Famine years, the crop failed completely. Sickness in the district was treated in the Dispensary at Enniskerry by John Gason M.D., who in 1835 had been practicing there for twenty years, and was now aged forty-two. He was also attached to the fever hospital in the village. He was a trained surgeon, physician and obstetrician, although there was also a mid-wife in the district who tended to most births. Gason was interviewed by the Poor Inquiry Commissioners in 1835.[37] He reported that the dispensary was open to the sick poor on Monday, Wednesday and Friday mornings between 10 and 12. The doctor was also able to visit those who could not attend within a circumference of 21 miles. There was also a nurse, who had been employed for the previous seven years, replacing her predecessor who was 'removed on account of drunkenness'. Until the Medical Charities Act, 1851, the dispensary was supported by the county Grand Jury an annual subscription of £1 1s from those in the district who could afford it. After 1851, healthcare was organised by dispensary districts in Poor Law unions, funded by the Poor Law Rate, paid by property owners.[38]

Gason considered the greatest cause of sickness in the village was due to the continued use of improper food, saying that 'many cases of dyspepsia and gastrodynia are clearly referable to a cold, washy, vegetable diet'. A Poor Fund in the village which provided some wine and additional dietary needs to the poor who were sick in their own houses or in the hospital. Gason considered the condition of clothes, food, bedding and furniture in the houses of the poor was 'in many cases indifferent, but generally speaking of a better description than in many parts of Ireland'.

The fever hospital was established in the village in 1814 for the treatment of infectious diseases, and had accommodation for fifteen men and fifteen women. As with the dispensary, it was supported by subscriptions and donations, and received an income of £141 in 1838 (£47 subscriptions and donations, £94 presentments) and £150 in each of the years 1845 and 1852 (£50 subscriptions and donations, £100 presentments). The expenditure of the hospital in 1853 was £165.[39] The most common fever was typhoid fever, which Gason considered was more prevalent in this district than elsewhere. In the decade 1831–1841, 456 males and 470 females were admitted to the hospital, with twenty-one male and sixteen female deaths in this time; a mortality rate of 1 in 25.[40] This was substantially better than mortality rates in other hospitals in the county – for example Bray (697 admissions), Newtown Mount Kennedy (827 admissions) and Arklow (1472 admissions) all had mortality rates of 1 in 20. In the period 1841–1851, the hospital 496 males and 394 females were admitted, with twenty-eight male and twenty-three female deaths recorded in this period – a mortality rate of 1 in 17.5. In this period, the rates for Bray (692 admissions) and Arklow (2,066 admissions) were 1 in 25 and 1 in 36 respectively. The 1851 census recorded the annual receptions and deaths for every hospital. The intake in 1847 (194) was almost double the average for the rest of the decade. The winter of 1847 was particularly harsh, and may have led to this higher intake. By 1861, the previous decade had seen 395 admissions with eight deaths, six from fever and two from other causes.[41] By 1871, the hospital had closed. It was subsequently used as a residence for employees of Powerscourt, and as a temporary schoolhouse for Enniskerry before becoming the Estate Office.

POST-FAMINE LIFE

In the aftermath of the Famine, life in the district moved on. As discussed, the population of the area declined, with a consequent decline in the number of 4th class houses, and a resultant easing of the pressure on the land. The Guardians of Powerscourt employed locals to build roads and engage in improvements works on the estate. With the majority of the 7th Viscount, employment was made available through the construction of the great terraces and gardens at Powerscourt House. A reflection on life before and after the Famine is given Mervyn, 7th Viscount, who was born in 1836:[42]

Even in my own lifetime I remember when there were perhaps fifteen to twenty families living in poverty in Glencree, where there are now three of four comfortable farmers who have each enough land to live upon, and whereas when I was a boy I recollect there being a soup kitchen in the farmyard and another in Enniskerry, where I have seen a crowd coming for soup provided by my family; now there is no distress, no soup kitchen and no necessity for it.

Employment in the area was still dominated by agriculture and labour. Buoyed by post-Famine rental income up to the mid-1870s, Powerscourt employed a large number of labourers and undertook a lot of development work on the demesne and the estate. Salary books and workmen's account books give some indication on the nature of the workforce and their duties. The books for 1850 list twenty men, and include among their list a payment to Saul Messett for driving the school car.[43] The books of 1855 list the thirty-three staff on the estate (not including house staff).[44] Men were paid 7-8*s* per week for six days' work. The work carried out each day is listed for every day except Sunday for the entire year. The work followed the seasons, so that a typical labourers duties by month from January would have been drawing manure, coal and straw, ploughing in January, working on the Tinnehinch road in February, drawing timber, turnips, ploughing and harrowing in March, drawing top dressing, rolling grass in April, drawing stones, drawing manure, ploughing and harrowing in May, drawing stones, drilling harrow in June, drawing gravel, mowing and weeding in July, making hay and reaping oats in August, reaping oats, making and taking in hay in September, threshing oats, drawing hay, digging potatoes and taking stuff off roads in October, digging potatoes, working on roads in November, drawing gravel, straw and leaves in December. There was one day off for Christmas day. Some of the workers had other responsibilities – for example bringing sheep to Dublin or going to Kingstown with luggage. In 1863, there were twenty-four labourers listed, each earning 8–10*s* per week[45] and by 1871 the numbers on the books was seasonal, with fifteen in winter and forty-seven in peak times. Payment was about 10–11*s* per week, and was increased to 15*s* during harvest time.

During this time, Powerscourt also invested in the building of new cottages for his labourers. Several designs were considered, including those from the English Cottage Improvement Society.[46] Powerscourt settled on plans from the Board of Works, but tells a story of why he subsequently changed the style of these in later developments:[47]

Outside Kilmolin Gate, I built eight blocks of labourers cottages. The first were constructed after a plan from the Board of Works, but they were rather large for labourers, two storeys high, and these are now inhabited by a mason, a carpenter, etc. The next two blocks were also built two stories high, one half of each cottage being a kitchen with an open roof; the other half divided into two bedrooms on the ground floor, and two over them, with an open wooden staircase in the kitchen leading to the upper bedrooms. Some years after these were built I went into one of them and remarked that the staircase had disappeared. On inquiring what had become of it, the occupants said: 'Ah! Sure we burnt it for firewood long ago!' I said: 'Then how do you get to the upper rooms?' 'Ah! Sure the fowls live up there!' After that I did not build and more two-storied cottages. The county councils now require that certain sanitary accommodation should be provided for each cottage, in a small separate building in the backyard: we complied with sanitary regulations, but I find that these structures are generally used for hen-roosts, or more commonly for storing potatoes in, instead of the purpose intended.

SUMMARY

After the population surge in the early part of the nineteenth century, the impact of poverty in the 1830s and the Famine in the 1840s resulted in a population decrease over the century from a peak of over 4,500 in 1831 to just over 1,500 in 1901. During this time, the proportion of people in the parish living in the village increased from about 6 per cent to around 15 per cent. The quality of housing stock improved, so that by 1861, virtually all fourth-class housing had been eliminated. The population of women in the parish, mirroring the north of the county reduced more dramatically as women went to work in domestic service in the city. Employment in the parish was primarily in agriculture. The practices in agriculture changed as the century progressed, with fewer, larger farms towards the end of the century. There were also some other employment opportunities on Powerscourt Estate. After the shock and devastation of the Famine – ameliorated somewhat by the proximity of Dublin, the efforts of a local Relief Committee and competent medical practitioners and facilities – the village enjoyed a renewed development phase coinciding with the majority of the 7th Viscount resulting in new roads, bridges, churches and housing. As development slowed by the 1870s, life in the village would have continued in a steady rhythm, remaining relatively unchanged until well into the new century.

APPENDIX

Below is a reproduction of Initial Application for Curtlestown School
to Board of Education
'Fitting Up of Schools' Form.

Curtlestown School–Roll #1119 Initial Application, 9 July 1834: ED1/95 No. 18
Co. Wicklow, District 40 & 38

QUERIES
TO BE ANSWERED BY APPLICANTS FOR AID TOWARDS THE FITTING-UP OF SCHOOLS, THE PAYING OF TEACHERS, AND THE OBTAINING OF SCHOOL REQUISITES

The Answers are expected to refer, not to what may be the present rules of conducting the school, but to the mode it is intended to conduct it, in the event of its receiving aid from the Board.

1. What is the name of the school and when was it established?
Curtlestown, established in the year 1818. [the 'r' in Curtlestown looks like a 't']
2. In what Townland, Parish and County is it situated?
Curtlestown, Powerscourt parish, Co. Wicklow.
3. What is the name and distance of the nearest Post-Town, and in what direction?
Enniskerry, two miles distant.
4. State, particularly, whether the school is, or has been, in connexion with or has derived aid from any other society – and if so, the name of the society, the amount

of aid received and the nature of the connexion, and whether that connexion is to continue?

Neither is nor has been in connexion with ... nor has derived aid from any other society.

5. State whether the school house is attached to, or erected upon, church or chapel ground?

Erected upon chapel ground but not attached to the chapel.

Of what material is it built?

Lime and stone.

Is it thatched or slated?

Slated.

What are its dimensions?

37 ½ feet by 13.

From what funds was it erected?

By local subscription.

Is the whole house exclusively employed for scholars?

Yes.

If not, who else uses it or dwells therein?

No person.

What is the number of rooms used as schoolrooms, and their dimensions?

All one room.

In what state of repair is the school house?

In good repair.

What number of desks and seats are there in the school room, and how many children do they accommodate?

16 seats, 70 ?feet? of desk sufficient to accommodate 150 children.

6. What are the sources from where the annual income of the school is derived, and what is the amount of such income – do the scholars pay anything and what?

No annual income the school was pay granting whatever they can afford but there are 40 free.

7. What arrangement is made respecting the imparting of religious instruction to the children? State particularly what day or days of the week are set apart for that purpose, and what hour or hours on any other day? State also whether public notification is given of this arrangement and whether parents are left at liberty to withhold their children from religious instruction which they do not approve of?

Saturday is set apart for imparting religious instruction [crossed out: given on Thursdays and Fridays from two to four o'clock ?Roll?] possible notification is given of this arrangement and parents are at liberty to withhold their children.

8. How many days in each week are employed in instructing the children in the common branches of moral and literary education and how many hours in each day? And state particularly at what hour the school commences and when it closes?

Five days in each week [crossed out: Saturday excepted] five hours each day [crossed out:

except the day on which religious instruction is given] School commences at ten o'clock and closes at three.

9. Is a register kept in the school, recording the daily attendance of the children and the average attendance of each week and each quarter?
Yes.

10. How many children have been present on the average every week for the last quarter of a year?
From 90 to 105, 70 males, 35 female.

11. Do you expect any increase and to what extent?
Great increase.

12. Are you disposed to use the books prepared and issued by the board? If not, state the titles of those books which you propose to use?
Yes.

13. State the names of the present teacher or teachers?
William Cosgrove.
Have they been educated at any model school?
Yes.
What testimonials can they produce of fitness for their office?
Very good testimonials.
What is the amount of salaries paid to them, and whence derived?
No salary except what the children pay.

14. Have the clergymen of the different denominations in the Parish, or in the neighbourhood of the school, been applied to in order to obtain their signatures to this application?
Yes they said they would not sign it.

15. Is the school under the direction of any individual or individuals or a committee? State the name and address of the individual or individuals – if a committee, state the name of the Treasurer, Secretary or Correspondent and HIS POST-TOWN?
Under the direction of the Revd Patrick Black, Curtlestown, post town Enniskerry.

16. What other schools are within three miles of yours, State their names, particularly whether national schools, and at what distance they are. State also under what patronage and direction they are.
Three schools not national schools within three miles nearest half a mile under the direction of the protestant rector.

17. What is the population of the parish?
Not yet ?ascertained?

18. Are there any persons, resident in Dublin, acquainted with the manager or the circumstances of this school? If so, state the name and address.
[Added in different ink, same as signature below: L. ?Fitzsimon? Cpn ---- Glencullen, Golden Ball]

19. Will a copy of the lesson contained in the regulations, No. VI be hung up conspicuously in the school, and the import of it carefully inculcated on the children? *Yes.*

20. Will access be given to the clergy of every denomination to enter the school room as visitors, provided they take no part in the business of the school, or interrupt it? *Yes .*

The nature and extent of the aid requested is as follows:

A salary for the master and school books.

We the undersigned, request the above aid from the Commissioners of National Education, believing the queries to be fully and truly answered, and engaging that the school shall be conducted according to the regulations set forth in our answers:

Protestants	**Roman Catholics**
Mrs Grattan	? Roche(?) PP
Rich Burton	Patrick Black CC
William Quigley	L. Fizsimmon(?)
Wingfield Burtton(?)	Thaddeus Callag(?) Gray
Joseph Burton	Seamus(?) Dixon
Timothy Quigley	M. Callagherry
Abraham Williams	John Mcannsey(?)
? Evans(?)	Bryan Ryder

Note added at back: SC 9/7 £10 salary from 1 April 16/7 [illegible]

Population of Townlands of Parish of Powerscourt 1841–1901 [1, 2, 3, 4, 5, 6, 7, 8, 9]

★Includes the population of the Glencree Reformatory from 1861

	1841	1851	1861	1871	1881	1891	1901
Annacrivey	302	167	139	74	57	52	39
Aurora★	126	113	336	411	378	337	253
Bahana	81	63	68	70	48	39	31

Ballinagee	91	71	66	57	61	42	40
Ballybrew	119	97	57	55	45	50	46
Ballycoyle	82	38	25	24	25	18	13
Ballylerane	22	20	23	21	18	11	12
Ballyreagh	73	73	34	35	39	24	13
Ballyross	96	98	73	70	42	39	34
Barnamire	91	74	40	47	56	50	36
Cloon	185	111	54	50	42	44	32
Cookstown	122	107	90	109	116	118	97
Crone	17	24	23	28	14	4	11
Curtlestown Lwr	19	15	29	27	13	10	12
Curtlestown Upr	19	20	4	5	2	6	2
Deerpark	44	40	21	30	32	25	15
Glaskenny	37	33	21	22	9	7	12
Killegar	166	202	217	144	118	131	114
Kilmalin	215	149	136	197	191	125	130
Knockbawn	10	6	11	8	7	5	6
Lackandarragh Lwr	37	13	14	13	21	15	13

Lackandarragh Upr	54	26	21	23	25	22	15
Monastery	141	115	69	89	67	72	77
Oldboleys	100	118	90	59	56	62	49
Onagh	33	13	15	12	15	15	9
Powerscourt Mountain	23	30	12	31	12	19	4
Powerscourt Demesne	103	43	52	65	75	78	60
Toneygarrow	160	105	109	79	79	72	63

List of Wellwishers at Retirement Function for Robert Sandys, Friday, 3 January 1845:

Rathdowne, DL, JP, Charleville
Robert Kennedy, Clk, Powerscourt Glebe
Arthur Edwards, Clk, Enniskerry
Capt Clifford Trotter, Charleville Cottage
Patrick Flood, Summerhill, Enniskerry
Christopher Russell, MD, Enniskerry
John Barrington, Enniskerry
John Williams, Ballybrew
William Sandys, Cookstown, Enniskerry
William Patrickson, Killegar, Enniskerry
Capt. Thomas Tierney, Calgary, Enniskerry
Edward Keegan, Ballinagee
Benjamin Buckley, Parknasilloge, Enniskerry
Thomas Buckley, Monastry, Enniskerry
Charles Strong, Monastry, Enniskerry
John Buckley, Balybrew, Enniskerry
William Harricks, Onagh, Enniskerry
Henry Keegan, Bahana, Enniskerry
Richard Burton, Annacrevy, Enniskerry

Thomas Murray, Cookstown, Enniskerry
William Williams, Cookstown, Enniskerry
Thomas Walker, Coolakey, Enniskerry
Joseph Burton, Barnamire, Enniskerry
Robert Buckley, Glaskenny, Enniskerry
Francis Buckley, Lackindarra, Enniskerry
Richard Buckley, Monastry, Enniskerry
James Quigley, Kilmolin, Enniskerry
Joseph Keegan, Monastry, Enniskerry
Edward Ward, Parknasellogue, Enniskerry
Richard Buckley, Enniskerry
Michael McGinty, Powerscourt, Enniskerry
John Buckley, Knockbawn, Enniskerry
Robert Williams, Ballybrew, Enniskerry
James Dixon, Enniskerry

(Placenames spelled as given.)

Henry Sandys Papers (National Library of Ireland MS 28,849(1))

NOTES

Chapter 1

1. Price, L. *Place Names of County Wicklow: Barony of Rathdown* Vol.V (1967)
2. Richard Wingfield was 1st Vicount Powerscourt (of the 3rd creation) from 1744 to 1751. The 1st and 2nd creations in 1618 (Richard Wingfield) and 1665 (Folliot Wingfield) were extinct on the death of the holders due to lack on an heir
3. Rocque, J. *An Actual Survey of the County of Dublin* (1760)
4. Prunty, J. *Maps and Map-Making in Local History* (Dublin: Four Courts Press, 2004)
5. Derrick, S. *Letters written from Leverpoole, Chester, Corke, the Lake of Killarney, Dublin, Tunbridge Wells, Bath* (London: Davis & Reymers, 1767)
6. Young, A. *A Tour in Ireland with General Observations on the State of that Kingdom, 1776, 1777 and 1778. And Brought Down to the End of 1779* (2nd ed.) (London: H. Goldney for T. Cadell, 1780)
7. Lease of house known as Tinnehinch Inn with land in Cookstown, (1780) MS 43003 (6), Powerscourt Papers, National Library of Ireland, Dublin
8. Curran, M. (1788). A map of part of Tinnehinch Co. Wicklow. MS 26,949, National Library of Ireland, Dublin
9. Bowden, C.T. *A tour through Ireland* (Dublin: Corbet, 1791)
10. Twiss, R. *A tour in Ireland in 1775 with a map and a view of the Salmon Leap at Ballyshannon* (London: Robson, 1776)
11. Anonymous 'A trip Through Part of the County of Wicklow in July 1791' *Walkers' Hibernian Magazine*, May No. 445 (1793)
12. Tyner, G., & Taylor, A. *The Traveller's Guide Through Ireland: Being an Accurate and Complete Companion to Capt. Alexander Taylor's Map of Ireland* (P. Byrne, 1794)
13. Seward, W.W. *The Topography of Ireland Ancient and Modern* (Dublin: Alexander Stewart, 1797)

14. The 1641 Depositions, held in Trinity College Dublin Library, include a testament from John Johnson, an innkeeper who lived in 'Kilgarren', in the parish of 'Stagonan' (Stagonil – the old name for the parish). See http://1641.tcd.ie/

15. Seward, W.W. *The Topography of Ireland Ancient and Modern* (Dublin: Alexander Stewart, 1797)

16. Wright, G.N. *A Guide to the County of Wicklow* (2nd ed.) (London: Baldwin, Craddock and Joy, 1827)

17. Abstract of answers and returns, pursuant to act 55 Geo. 3, for taking an account of population of Ireland in 1821, H.C. 1824 [577] xxii, p. 128

18. National Inventory of Architectural Heritage. from www.buildingsofireland.ie

19. Wingfield, M.E. *A Description and History of Powerscourt* (London: Mitchell & Hughes, 1903)

20. A reproduction of this painting is available as a postcard from the National Gallery of Ireland, Dublin

21. McCormick, A.E. Scrapbook of A.E. McCormick including original sketches and topographical prints, TX 4063 (1815–1840), National Library of Ireland, Dublin

22. Brocas, S.F. Enniskerry Bridge Co. Wicklow (No. 6), TX 1997 (6), National Library of Ireland, Dublin (1820-1847)

23. Brocas, S.F. The Moss House, Enniskerry Co. Wicklow (No. 22), TX 1997 (22) (1820-1847), National Library of Ireland, Dublin

24. Brocas, S.F. Grattan's House, Tinnehinch, Enniskerry, Co. Wicklow (No. 11), TX 1997 (11) (1820-1847), National Library of Ireland, Dublin

25. Blackhouse, between Kilmalin and Curtlestown, is noted on both of the Neville maps, but did not progress onto the Ordnance Survey maps. Similarly, Eelford/Ellford near Killegar, is noted on Neville and Rocque's maps, but did not progress onto the Ordnance Survey. Both names were in common use by people in the locality however, as they appear regularly in parish records well into the nineteenth century

26. The actual date of this map is uncertain, it is most likely *c.* 1798 or later

27. Fewer, M., *The Wicklow Military Road* (Dublin: Ashfield Press, 2007)

28. A map of part of the old roads and new intended road leading from the old road at the upper end of Glencree by Lough Bray to the road of Shramamuck and Adowne (1799). MS 21F 163/43, National Library of Ireland, Dublin

29. Duncan, W. Map attached to lease for Glencree Barracks and land (1802). MS 43010/1 Powerscourt Papers, National Library of Ireland, Dublin

30. Lewis, S. *A Topographical Dictionary of Ireland* (London: S. Lewis & Co., 1837)

31. Sheehy, J. (1992). 'Powerscourt and Enniskerry: The Architectural Development of an Estate', in A. Bernelle (ed.), *Decantations: A Tribute to Maurice Craig* (Dublin: Lilliput, 1992), pp. 213

32. The story of the Bray and Enniskerry Railway is told in Liam Clare's book of the same name

33. Ordnance Survey Boundary Remark Books 159 (1-2), Book 1, OS 55 Boundary Remark Books, National Archives, Dublin

34. Areas converted from acres, roods and perches. There are 40 perches in a rood and 40 roods in an acre. 100 hectare (ha) is equal to 247 acres or 1 km^2

35. Brocas, S.F. At Enniskerry, 15 June, TX 1999 (6) (1820-1847), National Library of Ireland, Dublin

36. The 1851 census reports that the Fever Hospital in Enniskerry opened in 1814

37. Willis, N.P., Coyne, J.S., & Bartlett, W.H. *The Scenery and Antiquities of Ireland* (London: G. Virtue, 1842)

38. Hall, S.C. *Ireland, Its Scenery and Character &c.* (London: How & Parsons, 1841-3)

39. Sheehy, J. (1992). 'Powerscourt and Enniskerry: The Architectural Development of an Estate', in A. Bernelle (ed.), *Decantations: A Tribute to Maurice Craig* (Dublin: Lilliput, 1992), pp. 213

40. *ibid*

41. Valuation Office Enniskerry House Book (1840) 5.3573 Valuation Office House Books, National Archives of Ireland, Dublin

42. *ibid*

43. National Inventory of Architectural Heritage from www.buildingsofireland.ie

44. Valuation Office Enniskerry House Book (1840) 5.3573 Valuation Office House Books, National Archives of Ireland, Dublin

45. Office was a generic term for outhouse or any building of an industrial nature

46. Cash, G. The well in the Old Mill at Inniskerry, Co. Wicklow, TA 1839, National Library of Ireland, Dublin

47. Brocas, S.F. Enniskerry bridge Co. Wicklow (No. 6), TX 1997 (6) (1820-1847), National Library of Ireland, Dublin

48. Wingfield, L. Powerscourt Photo Album, Album 16 (1863), National Photographic Archive, Dublin

49. Map and sections of present and proposed roads from Enniskerry to crossroads at Kilmolin, (No date) MS 21F 163/22, National Library of Ireland, Dublin

50. There are leases in the Powerscourt Papers, by Richard, 5th Viscount to Timothy Quigley 'for part of land of Kilgarron alias Knocksink for 3 lives or 31 years at an annual rent of £25' (MS 43011/4), to Margaret Dixon 'for part of lands at Kilgarron for 3 lives or 31 years at an annual rent of £17 1s 3d' (MS 43012/1) and by Richard, 6th Viscount 'for lands of Barnasillogue otherwise Parknasillock to Edward Ward for 3 lives or 31 years at an annual rent of £13' (MS 43013/3). A subsequent lease to Timothy Quigley dated 1842 is also present (MS 43014/2), and Quigley was also a signatory on the 1834 application for Curtlestown School to become a National School

51. There are leases in the Powerscourt Papers, by Richard, 5th Viscount to Francis Miller (MS 43011/9) and James Miller (MS 43011/10) for lands at Monastery for rents of £5 each. Griffith also mentions several Millers as lessees in his valuation

52. Map showing plans for improvements of road near Waterfall (1834) MS 21F163 (65), National Library of Ireland, Dublin

53. Design for New Bridge and proposed line of road from near entrance gate to Powerscourt Waterfall leading towards Bahana (no date) MS 21F163 (64), National Library of Ireland, Dublin

54. Design for two new bridges – Bridge near waterfall and Bridge on double stream on upper part of new road (1847) MS 21F163 (67), National Library of Ireland, Dublin

55. Wingfield, M.E. *A Description and History of Powerscourt* (London: Mitchell & Hughes, 1903)

56. Workmen's Accounts Book, Powerscourt Estate (1855) MS 3165 (64), Powerscourt Papers, National Library of Ireland, Dublin

57. Wingfield, M.E. *A Description and History of Powerscourt* (London: Mitchell & Hughes, 1903)

58. Dooley, T. *The Decline of the Big House in Ireland* (Dublin: Wolfhound Press, 2001)

59. 'Great Fire at Enniskerry' *Freeman's Journal* (24 December 1894)

Chapter 2

1. Second report of the commissioners of Irish education inquiry H.C. 1826-7 [12] xii, Appendix 22, p. 850

2. First report of the Commissioners of Irish Education Inquiry, H.C. 1825 [400] xii, Appendix No. 258, p. 798

3. Second report of the commissioners of Irish education inquiry H.C. 1826-7 [12] xii, Appendix 22, p. 850

4. The returns stated whether Protestant children were in the Established Church, Presbyterian or of other Protestant denominations. All children in these returns were in the Established Church, so other churches are left out of this table for clarity; the amount paid by Lord Powerscourt to Cookstown School is not given

5. First report of the Commissioners of Public Instruction, Ireland, H.C. 1835 [45, 46, 47] xxxiii, p. 112b

6. First report of the Commissioners of Irish Education Inquiry, H. C. 1825 [400] xii, Appendix No. 220, p. 550

7. Parkes, S.M. *A Guide to the Sources for the History of Irish Education 1780-1922* (Dublin: Four Courts Press, 2010)

8. From the context, it is assumed that anxiety is meant with a sense of eagerness or desire

9. First report of the Commissioners of Irish Education Inquiry, H.C. 1825 [400] xii, Appendix No. 220, p. 550

10. Parkes, S.M. *A Guide to the Sources for the History of Irish Education 1780-1922* (Dublin: Four Courts Press, 2010)

11. First report of the Commissioners of Irish Education Inquiry, H.C. 1825 [400] xii, Appendix No. 217, p. 542

12.   *ibid*

13.   First report of the Commissioners of Irish Education Inquiry, H.C. 1825 [400] xii,
       Appendix No. 258, p. 798

14.   Parkes, S.M. *A Guide to the Sources for the History of Irish Education 1780-1922* (Dublin:
       Four Courts Press, 2010)

15.   ED1/95 (18), ED1 (1835), National Archives of Ireland, Dublin

16.   National Board of Education County Wicklow (183 -1855) ED2/49 (23), ED2,
       National Archives of Ireland, Dublin

17.   National Board of Education District 40 Vol. I (1855-1878) ED2/156 (16), ED2,
       National Archives of Ireland, Dublin

18.   National Board of Education District 38 Vol. I (1879-1880) ED2/151 (18), ED2,
       National Archives of Ireland, Dublin

19.   National Board of Education District 40 Vol. II, (1887-1902) ED2/157 (64), ED2,
       National Archives of Ireland, Dublin

20.   ED1/95 (108), ED1, (*c.* 1862) National Archives of Ireland, Dublin

21.   ED1/95 (96), ED1, (1863) National Archives of Ireland, Dublin

22.   ED1/97 (52), ED1, (1875) National Archives of Ireland, Dublin

23.   Lord Viscount Powerscourt's Servants Wages (1844) MS 43038/3 Powerscourt Papers,
       National Library of Ireland, Dublin

24.   Voucher for work completed (1846) MS 43046/3 Powerscourt Papers, National
       Library of Ireland, Dublin

25.   ED1/97 (6), ED1, (1867) National Archives of Ireland, Dublin

26.   National Board of Education District 40 Vol. II (1867-1878) ED2/157 (4), ED2,
       National Archives of Ireland, Dublin

27.   National Board of Education District 38 Vol. II (1879-1882) ED2/151 (34), ED2,
       National Archives of Ireland, Dublin

28.   National Board of Education District 40 Vol. II (1890-1899) ED2/157 (83), ED2,
       National Archives of Ireland, Dublin

29.   Third report of the commissioners of manual and practical instruction in primary schools
       under the Board of National Education in Ireland, H.C. 1897 [8618, 8619] xliii, p. 66

30.   Third report of the commissioners of Irish education inquiry H.C. 1836 [44] xxxvi, p.
       44

31.   Sixty-fifth report of the commissioners of Irish education inquiry H.C. 1899 [C.9446]
       xxiv Appendix, p. 246

32.   Report of the Commissioners appointed to take the census of Ireland for the year
       1841, H.C. 1843 [504] xxiv, p. 140

33.   The census of Ireland for the year 1861 part ii: Report and tables on ages and
       education Vol. i, H.C. 1863 [3204-I] lvi, p. 324

34.   The census of Ireland for the year 1861 part ii: Report and tables on ages and
       education Vol. i, H.C. 1863 [3204-I] lvi, p. xxxvii (errata)